Communication Theory & Research Applications

Communication Theory & Research Applications

Michael W. Singletary and Gerald Stone

IOWA STATE UNIVERSITY PRESS • AMES

Michael W. Singletary is professor of journalism, College of Communications, University of Tennessee, Knoxville, Tennessee.

Gerald Stone is professor of journalism, Department of Journalism, Memphis State University, Memphis, Tennessee.

© 1988 Iowa State University Press, Ames, Iowa 50010
All rights reserved.

Composed and printed in the United States of America

Questionnaires, coding forms, and overhead projection forms may be copied as needed for use in classroom exercises. Other materials should not be copied, stored in a retrieval system, or transmitted in any form or by any means without permission from the publisher.

First edition, 1988

Library of Congress Cataloging-in-Publication Data

Singletary, Michael W., 1938-
    Communication theory and research applications / Michael W. Singletary, Gerald Stone.—1st ed.
      p.   cm.
  ISBN 0-8138-0298-9
    1. Communication—Philosophy. 2. Communication—Research. 3. Communication—Methodology. I. Stone, Gerald, 1944-
II. Title.
P91.S47   1988
001.51′01—dc19   87-38061
                                                                               CIP

Contents

Preface   *vii*

PART ONE *Relating Theory to Media Practice*

1.	Media Use: A Questionnaire	3
2.	Media Use: Measuring "Use"	7
3.	Media Use: Opinion Leadership	11
4.	Media Use: Examining the Questions	14
5.	Selected Models of Communication	16
6.	News Choices: Gatekeeping	22
7.	Propaganda: Characteristics and Practice	26
8.	News Styles	31
9.	Bias and Stereotypical Portrayals	38
10.	The Knowledge Gap	43
11.	Theory of Relative Constancy	47
12.	Attitudes and Attitude Change	53

PART TWO *Selected Theories and Hypotheses*

13.	The Rise and Fall of Communication Theories	61
14.	Message Factors in Persuasion	65
15.	Source Credibility	69
16.	Group Dynamics	74
17.	Diffusion of Information	75
18.	Diffusion of Innovation	80
19.	Agenda Setting	84
20.	The Cultivation Hypothesis	90
21.	Media Uses and Gratifications	96
22.	Socialization	100
23.	Coorientation	108
24.	Nonhuman Communication	111
25.	Prosocial and Antisocial Learning	113
26.	Spiral of Silence	118

PART THREE *Some Research Methods in Communication Theory*

27.	Knowing Research Terms	123
28.	Critiquing the Data of Theory	130
29.	The .05 Level of Significance	135
30.	Journal Synopses	141
31.	Sampling, Sampling Distribution, Sampling Error	144

32.	Questionnaire Design	155
33.	Readability	160
34.	Content Analysis	168
35.	Reliability of Measurements in Content Analysis	174
36.	Semantic Differential	179
37.	Q Methodology in Social Research	184
38.	AAPOR Guidelines	187
39.	Choice of Interviewing Method	189
40.	Validity of Measures	193
41.	Experimental Design	197

Index   205

Preface

The first course in communication theory and research can be both a memorable and an exasperating experience for students. On the one hand, it is an eye-opening revelation that so much thought and research has been done by such a wide variety of scholars. On the other hand, it is extremely difficult to try to synthesize the material--to link the multitude of concepts and make any sense of the whole. Making matters worse for students is the lack of opportunity to work with the vast quantity of material presented. Learning is more difficult and less enjoyable if it involves a lot of memorization.

The authors have been teaching communication theory and research for more than 20 years. They have watched the perplexed stares and heard the querulous "but what good is it?" enough times to appreciate the need for a hands-on approach. In fact, there is a strong suspicion that anyone teaching an effective course in mass communication theory or research has already discovered how much more learning takes place if students can be shown, rather than just told, some of the concepts they are being taught. Even a weak example, if it furthers student participation and involvement with the concept, is superior to no example.

This text approaches theory and research with both the teacher and the student in mind. For the student, there are important readings, supplemented by understandable narratives, supplemented in turn by (and this is a key point) hands-on opportunities to work with theory. Each chapter includes a research project or some other activity designed to drive home and clarify the topic being discussed. For the teacher, this approach allows the flexibility to expand a section to any depth. This will be very important to instructors who build their courses around readings and lectures. For instructors who use a survey text, our book may serve as a supplement.

These hands-on examples of theory and research concepts have proven themselves in class at the undergraduate and graduate levels. They have been evaluated by students based on the ability of the exercises to clarify the concept and have received rave reviews. They work. They will add the practical dimension to the subject of mass communication theory and research. And, most important, they will enhance the learning experience.

A teachers' manual is available, which provides instructional background for using some of the exercises. While students will have in this book the pages they need to work from, the manual will help instructors present these lessons in a step-by-step manner, pointing out potential pitfalls that might occur along the way. The teachers' manual also offers many more in-class exercises that the instructors may want to present--

examples that support the concepts in the text but that will be most effective if instructors present them in class without having the students follow along in their own books.

The authors are indebted to their teaching colleagues who have suggested some of these examples through the years. They are most indebted to their students who have unknowingly served as test-market subjects for these lessons and through whose feedback the lessons have been improved to the extent that they are now being shared with others.

Readers are invited to write to the authors with suggestions for improving or expanding these exercises or the suggested readings.

PART ONE

Relating Theory to Media Practice

UNIT 1

Media Use: A Questionnaire

READING:
Shearon A. Lowery and Melvin L. De Fleur. "The People's Choice: The Media in a Political Campaign." *Milestones in Mass Communication Research*, 2d ed. New York: Longman, 1988, pp. 79-103.

This unit involves completion of a media-use questionnaire. Turn to the questionnaire at the end of this unit and answer the questions on both pages. Do that before reading further; the questionnaire should require only about 5 to 8 minutes to complete.

Now we can begin to consider what the media-use questionnaire shows about people's use of media as reported through this self-administered device. We can first consider the source of many of these questions and why they were selected for use in charting your media habits.

Most of the items were used similarly by political science researchers Paul Lazarsfeld, Bernard Berelson, and Hazel Gaudet more than 40 years ago in a classic study of what influences a person's decision to vote for a particular candidate. Although it now seems difficult to imagine, it was not until the 1940 presidential election that researchers first thought to include the mass media as a possible influence on people's voting decisions. In fact, the three researchers just tossed a few media-use questions into a questionnaire that was going to be used in yet another survey of election influences, perhaps one better designed than those that had preceded it.

But the outcome was spectacular. Not only did the study result in an exceptional book, *The People's Choice*, which had several printings, but the three researchers became leaders in a newly established scientific discipline: mass communication research. Beyond these outcomes, the study provided the first real theory of mass communication, "The Two-Step Flow Theory," in which information disseminated by the mass media was received by opinion leaders in the general population who related the information to others in their social groups. Opinion leaders were the direct receivers of the message, and they shared certain demographic characteristics such as being better educated, in a slightly higher income category, and more gregarious than others in their social group. The "others" were classified as followers or "indirect receivers" who relied on their opinion leaders not only to provide information on a certain topic area but to interpret that information for them as well.

Naturally, some questions on media use have been added to this unit's questionnaire. There was no television in 1940; magazines were not available at grocery counter checkouts because there were no chain grocery stores as we know them now. Also, there is more detail on our media-use questionnaire because we include a question that seeks to determine levels of interest in a variety of news categories in a daily newspaper (question 2).

Our questionnaire also contains items (questions 17 to 21) that go beyond media use. The entire section on interaction with others is designed to elicit responses that could tap a person's general position in a social setting: opinion leader vs. follower. If you were asked this question, "Which kind of 'information person' would you say you are in relation to your group of friends: a leader or follower?" you would probably have a tough time deciding. Most people would. We can all think of topics on which we are the opinion leaders and of others on which we are followers. You might be the one in the group who decides which movie to see, but you might rely on the others for decisions on the best-fitting fashion jeans to purchase. Lazarsfeld, Berelson, and Gaudet didn't find that out in their survey, but later communication researchers who probed the topic further did.

Why did it take five different questions to tap the concept of opinion leader vs. follower? Unit 2 offers some answers.

EXERCISE

MEDIA-USE QUESTIONNAIRE

General Media Use:

1. How many days a week do you read a daily newspaper? _____

2. Which of the following items do you generally read when you do read a daily newspaper? (Check all that apply.)

   ____ international news ____ sports   ____ horoscopes, games,
   ____ national news   ____ editorials   or puzzles
   ____ local news   ____ letters to   ____ fashion or food
   ____ advertisements   editor   ____ classifieds
   ____ comics   ____ columnists   ____ other: weather,
                                                   socials, etc.

3. Do you read a weekly newspaper?   yes   no

4. How many days a week do you watch a local TV news show? _____

5. How many days a week do you watch a national TV news show? _____

6. Do you regularly read a weekly newsmagazine?   yes   no

7. How much time per day do you spend listening to radio? ___hr; ___min.

8. How much time do you spend daily listening to tapes, disks, and records? ___hr; ___min.

9. About how much time per day do you spend watching TV, including news? _____

10. How many times a month do you go out to a movie? _____
    a. Please list the last three movies you have seen _____
    _____

11. Do you receive cable TV?   yes   no

12. Do you regularly watch a weekly TV "magazine" format program?
    yes   no

13. Not counting textbooks, how many books have you read in the past year? _____

14. To how many magazines, of any type, do you subscribe? _____
    a. Please list them: _____
    _____

5

15. List the last several magazines that you remember scanning at a newsstand or grocery counter to which you do not subscribe:
   _____
   _____

16. Generally, compared with other Americans, would you say your media use is:

   more than average /___/___/___/___/___/___/ less than average

Interaction with Others:

17. To how many clubs or organizations do you now belong? _____

18. Excluding relatives, about how many people do you talk with per day, on average? ("Talk with" means more than casual greeting.) _____

19. Approximately how many times per day do you discuss current events or politics with others? _____

20. If you and friends disagree during a conversation, which of the following outcomes usually occurs? (Check only one.)

   ___You maintain your position until others agree with you.
   ___You continue your position and others maintain theirs.
   ___You give in but really aren't convinced.
   ___You begin to accept their arguments as valid.

21. Check your position under each of the following headings:

	Mostly You Advise Others	Mostly Others Advise You	Usually Goes Both Ways
a. On topics about new styles and fashion:	_____	_____	_____
b. On consumer matters such as food or auto repair products, etc., and where to shop:	_____	_____	_____
c. On political topics:	_____	_____	_____
d. On personal relationship topics:	_____	_____	_____
e. On current events:	_____	_____	_____

UNIT 2

Media Use: Measuring "Use"

READING:
David H. Weaver. "Estimating the Value of Newspaper Content for Readers: A Comparison of Two Methods." *Newspaper Research Journal* Prototype (April 1979):7-13.

Communication research is a difficult business. This is true because human beings are complex, probably the most complex research subject of all. Each of us is a mass of interwoven influences (biological, physiological, environmental, etc.). Most of us could not possibly say, based on a single question, whether we are information leaders or followers. There are a host of things about ourselves we probably couldn't or wouldn't answer if asked directly. So when a researcher is dealing with people and trying to gather information on some complex aspect of human nature, the best one can do is try to estimate the right answer.

One way to do that is through indexes. An index is a series of questions or scales that, when combined appropriately, form a continuum along which a person can be placed with regard to others who have completed the same items. An example is needed. Let's say you are asked simply, "Are you a good sleeper?" If you are an insomniac, you know you are a bad sleeper. But do the rest of us know what kind of sleepers we are? What constitutes an "average" sleeper? The way to go about determining if an individual should be placed in the good or bad sleeper category (and perhaps rank each along a continuum of sleeping habits) is to ask a series of questions each person can answer, which taken together would classify the person as a good or a bad sleeper:

1. About how many hours a night do you sleep, on average?
2. About how long does it take you to get to sleep?
3. Do you wake up during the night?
4. If you awaken, about how many times do you do so on an average night?
5. Do you occasionally take pills to help you sleep?
6. Do you often feel tired during the day?

The list of questions could be longer, or we might be able to correctly estimate sleeping habits by using only a few of the above. However, we would all agree that using all or most of the above questions would provide a more reliable answer than using only one. And the important thing here is that we all can answer the six questions without any difficulty.

Now, when we are satisfied that our series of questions is long enough, but not too long, and that the list is germane to the topic, we can feel fairly confident that the individual's series of responses to our scale will correctly classify the person as either a good or a bad sleeper. The way to continue is to convert the answer to these questions into numbers. If we get a "yes" to question 3, we could translate that to a zero, while a "no" can equal one. We would use that particular classification because we would probably want to designate the person scoring highest on the scale (the sum of scores) as the best sleeper. Maybe we would decide to award a point on the scale for every hour given as an answer to question 1: a person who sleeps eight hours would get eight more points on the scale; one who sleeps only six hours would get six points, etc. For question 2, "How long does it take you to get to sleep?" we would deduct a point for every 15 minutes above the first 15 because we might decide that an "average" person might require about that long to get to sleep.

We would continue on the above procedure of adding or deducting points based on our decisions of how the questions best identify sleeping habits, that is, how the questions might discriminate good from bad sleepers. All this sounds reasonable and proper. But remember, we are dealing with people. Consider the following:

1. Not everyone needs the same amount of sleep; six hours might be sufficient for many, but we are docking our six-hour sleepers two whole points.

2. If a person feels tired during the day on a regular basis, is it a lack of sleep, a lack of exercise, a dietary problem, a medical problem, or unrequited love?

3. If you awaken once during the night and we dock you a point for that, should we dock you only two points for awakening twice? Awakening once may be necessary for people with a small bladder, while twice may be a real sign of difficulty in sleeping. Perhaps you should be docked 10 points if you awaken more than twice during the night.

These are some of the difficulties we have when our subjects are human beings. We can never assume that people can be measured as if they are ounces of lead or rats in a maze. Our measuring instruments aren't that good, and human beings can't be trusted to react in exactly the same way a second time.

Although we have looked at ways to attempt to measure complex concepts (for example, "Are you a good sleeper?"), we have learned that when it comes to measuring people's behavior, including communications, we can only approximate. We have seen how to go about constructing an index from a series of questions and how the index may differentiate people along a continuum.

EXERCISE

Go back to the media-use questionnaire. List in the space provided below the concepts that are being scaled and identify the *scale items* (questions) that relate to each concept. Using the kind of point system we have suggested, compute scores for yourself on each of the concepts. If feasible, compare scores with another member of the class. If comparisons are to be made, be certain you and your partner have used the same point system! And notice also that the point system has to be persuasive to the critic. Discuss with your partner the degree to which the scores probably are an accurate reflection of communications behavior or to what extent the scales are inaccurate.

Concept 1. Example: Broadcast Media Use

    Item   4   _____

    Item   5   _____

    Item   7   _____

    Item   9   _____

    Item 12   _____

(Note: It is not necessary to list every question relevant to a concept.)

Concept 2. _____

    Item _____ _____

    Item _____ _____

    Item _____ _____

    Item _____ _____

    Item _____ _____

Concept 3. _____

    Item _____ _____

    Item _____ _____

    Item _____ _____

    Item _____ _____

    Item _____ _____

Concept 4. _____
    Item _____ _____
    Item _____ _____
    Item _____ _____
    Item _____ _____
    Item _____ _____

UNIT 3

Media Use: Opinion Leadership

READING:
Shearon A. Lowery and Melvin L. De Fleur. "Personal Influence: The Two Step Flow of Communication." *Milestones in Mass Communication Research*, 2d ed. New York: Longman, 1988, pp. 163-86.

Consider the Lazarsfeld, Berelson, and Gaudet finding that opinion leaders share certain characteristics such as higher education. The researchers also found a relationship between media use and opinion leadership. Generally speaking, the opinion leaders (particularly on political topics) tended to be more frequent users of the mass media than followers. We can't really test the correlation of education level and media use with a classroom sample because everyone will have about the same level of education; that is, the class is a relatively homogeneous group. But we can test the relationship between frequency of media use and opinion leadership in a person's social group, based on a brief analysis of responses to the questionnaire.

Our hypothesis is: *opinion leadership is related to the frequency of media use*. We can't say that more frequent media use causes a person to be an opinion leader, and in fact it may be the other way around; having an extrovert personality, which is a sign of opinion leadership under many conditions, may in fact lead a person to use the media more frequently. (Remember those commercials for *Time* and *Newsweek*? They sold their product under the premise that you could be the life of the party if you kept up on current events by reading newsmagazines.) So, though we can't prove that greater media use makes a person an opinion leader, we can at least see if the concepts are related.

EXERCISE

Let's get on with our hypothesis testing. Go back to your own media-use questionnaire. In the margin, give yourself one point for every day you reported reading a daily newspaper in question 1. Skip to question 3 and give yourself one point if you answered "yes" (no points if you answered "no"). Give yourself half a point for each day you marked on item 4, and another half-point for each day you marked on item 5. If you answered "yes" to item 6, give yourself three points. (Reading a newsmagazine regularly is a telltale sign of interest in public affairs and a sign that you use the media to keep abreast of current events). Give yourself one point for a "yes" on item 12. Give yourself half a point for each book you have read in the past year, item 13 (only half a point because some might have been romantic novels); don't give yourself any more than three points on item 13 even if you read 20 books in the past year (we don't want to give this item too much weight in the scale). Give yourself half a point for each magazine in item 14. Total all your points.

On the second page of the questionnaire, we can estimate your general *opinion leadership rating*. Give yourself one point for each five people you counted in item 18, up to a maximum of three points. Give yourself one point for each current events/political discussion per day numbered in item 19, up to a maximum of three points. If you said you maintain your position until others agree with you in item 20, give yourself four points. If you said in item 20 that you give in without being convinced, deduct one point from your score. If you said in item 20 you begin to accept their arguments as valid, deduct two points. For each part in item 21 that you've checked "mostly you advise others," give yourself one point. For each part that you have checked "mostly others advise you," deduct half a point. Total all your points.

You now have two tallies: one on frequency of media use and one on opinion leadership. Are they accurate? The counts should be accurate, but whether the counts correctly reflect your actual media-use frequency or opinion leadership status is debatable. Still, for the sake of the experiment, we will try to test the hypothesis. The data might be recorded as shown in Table 3.1.

Table 3.1. Opinion Leadership and Media Use

	Low Leadership	High Leadership
Low Media Use	I $n = 4$[a] 16%	II $n = 1$ 4%
High Media Use	III $n = 7$ 30%	IV $n = 12$ 50%

[a]Fictional data.

If a student scored below the mean in media use and below the mean in opinion leadership, the person would be counted in cell 1. If a student scored high in media use and low in opinion leadership, the person would be counted in cell 3. And so on, until everyone in class is in one of the four cells. One more operation may be helpful. Convert the frequencies (example, $n = 4$) to percentages. Simply divide the number in a cell by the total number of persons responding, in our case 24. Example: 4/24 = 16%. You are now ready to evaluate the hypothesis that media use is related to opinion leadership.

With any luck, the figures you obtain will be roughly like those in Table 3.1. Those in cell 1 should be higher than cell 2, and cell 4 should be higher than cell 3. If so, we have shown that even in class, where education may blur distinctions, low media use and low leadership go together, as do high media use and high leadership. If luck fails us, the opposite boxes may have the highest percentages. If that is the case, we can argue (sheepishly) that our weighting of the value of the answers on the questionnaire was inappropriate. But we would still have to declare the hypothesis unsupported.

UNIT 4
Media Use: Examining the Questions

READING:
Jean M. Converse and Stanley Presser. *Survey Questions: Handcrafting the Standardized Questionnaire*. Beverly Hills, Calif.: Sage, 1986, pp. 9-75.

As an exercise in critical analysis of research, let's consider more problems of the media-use questionnaire. You probably noticed some of these as you were filling out the form.

In the first question, are the respondents supposed to consider the Sunday newspaper part of the daily newspaper? They probably would, and if they read a newspaper every day including Sunday, they would answer the question with 7. But a few people might be waiting for a separate question about Sunday papers, and they might answer 6, although they should be including the Sunday paper if they read it. We could improve the question by adding "including the Sunday paper."

What do we mean by a weekly newspaper? In many smaller communities a weekly is the only paper. It contains news and news pictures, ads and classifieds--virtually the entire range of content found in most daily newspapers. This is the kind of newspaper the question is asking about. But there are a number of other weekly newspapers today: "shoppers" that contain only ads, "coupon" newspapers that come in the mail every week, "freely circulated" daily newspaper spinoff editions (called total market coverage papers), home-buying guides, used car-buying guides, and others. If you receive one of the others, you might have answered "yes" to item 3, although the kind of paper you would be talking about is not the same kind of weekly paper the question seeks to identify.

Similar problems exist with the two TV news items. Some local newscasts are only five minutes long in the early morning. Some local newscasts are half an hour, others are an hour, and some are even two hours. Do we count "newsbreaks" and other short national news segments as a regular national news show? Perhaps these items should have been clarified, or perhaps the questions would have been improved by asking how many hours a week do you spend watching a local TV news show?

Does everybody who listens to records really listen to them every day? Probably not. But the question forces respondents to report their estimated daily record listening time. Maybe it should have been, "How much time do you spend per week listening to records? (not on radio)." Does "records" include cassette tapes and compact disks?

What about item 10, part a? When asked about the last three movies you have seen, did you include movies shown on television? The question really seeks to tap movies you have seen in a theater. But it doesn't say that, does it?

EXERCISE

You should now continue scanning the questionnaire beginning with item 11 and see how many problems you can add to the list:

1.

2.

3.

4.

5.

UNIT 5
Selected Models of Communication

READING:
Bruce Westley and Malcolm MacLean. "A Conceptual Model for Communications Research." *Journalism Quarterly* 34(1957):31-38.

Model, as the term is used here, refers to the symbolic representation of communication processes. The model is a kind of characterization of what takes place when information is transmitted from point A to point B. Most plainly, the model is a picture of communication. But why would we need such a picture? Two reasons come quickly to mind. (1) Students of communication need to be reminded of the interrelated behaviors required for communication and (2) the model isolates individual parts of the communication process so that they can be examined separately.

One of the earliest mass communication models was what now seems a very simple question by Harold Lasswell: "Who says what, in which channel, to whom, with what effect?" Although the question is not graphic in the sense of the lines, arrows, and boxes that characterize later models, it serves the same purpose. It separates the communication process into parts, and it allows the student to examine each part separately. At the time Lasswell's famous question was published, the flower of mass communication research was hardly more than a bud; the Lasswell model was an important contribution, and it remains widely cited today.

Subsequent models of communication either focused on particular aspects of communication or attempted to expand the model to account for special circumstances. Over the years, there have been many models published; we will examine only a few.

THE INFORMATION MODEL

Shannon and Weaver used communication to mean "all the procedures by which one mind may affect another." Their work grew out of telephone engineering studies aimed at estimating the success and failure of transmission of large volumes of information. But they believed that their model (shown in Fig. 5.1) characterized communications in a very general way. They said communication could involve automatic electronic tracking equipment or individuals' speech communication, but the model could also be applied to music of any sort and to still or moving pictures, as in television. In short, they thought that their model of communication was encompassing, and indeed it was adopted for discussion in many mass communication textbooks over the years.

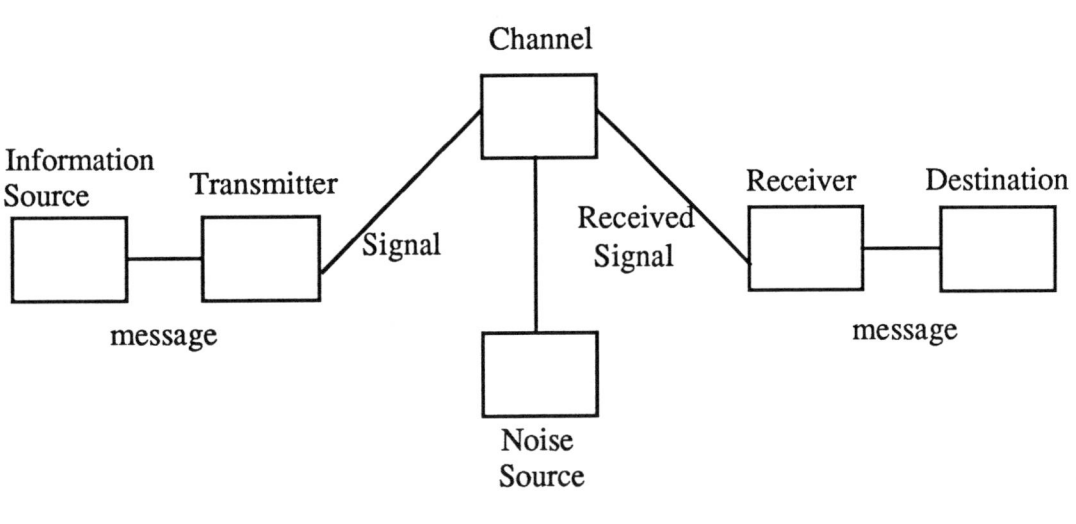

Fig. 5.1. Shannon-Weaver information model. Source: Claude E. Shannon and Warren Weaver. *The Mathematical Theory of Communication*. University of Illinois Press: Urbana, Ill., 1949. Used with permission.

Shannon and Weaver emphasized that the word "information" in this theory is used in a special sense and that it must not be confused with "meaning." Information referred to any bit of data.

They introduced the idea of *entropy* and *redundancy*. Entropy refers to uncertainty; redundancy to certainty. The goal of communication is to reduce entropy. Finally, "noise" increases entropy. Noise might be static, as in radio reception, or it might be a distracting manner of speech.

Now, armed with this very brief description of the model, ponder these questions:

1. Does the model characterize all the aspects of human and mass communication? Write your response here.

2. Does the model correspond closely enough to the practice of mass communication to be a useful analytical tool? Write your response here.

SOCIAL-PSYCHOLOGICAL MODEL

Whereas Shannon and Weaver's model was essentially mechanical, psychologists have emphasized interpersonal aspects. Particularly, they have focused on individuals' "strain toward symmetry." Symmetry refers to individuals' orientations toward an object. Let's say person A and person B are good friends, and their attention has been drawn to item C, which could be anything--a bicycle, a movie, an idea. Let's say that A likes C, but B does not. Given that A and B like each other, what happens to reduce the imbalance of the situation? If the bonds between A and B are strong enough, we could predict either that B will come to appreciate C, as does A, or B may decide that C is not really very important and so will mostly ignore the problem. In other words, efforts will be made to bring the situation into balance. This is a very simple kind of model, or theory, but a very powerful one. Surely, evidence of the strain toward symmetry is seen routinely if only we look. To reduce imbalance, or the threat of imbalance, we gather around us people who are largely like ourselves; our friends very likely share our values, goals, ideals, lifestyles, etc. And as we maintain our symmetric relationships, we simultaneously reinforce our conceptions of how things are and ought to be. ("Sure," we say, "here's how it is; and my friends can back me up!" We don't stop to think that our friends may be a poor sample, a sample selected in part to maintain interpersonal balance.)

The model is reproduced in Figure 5.2.

A likes B.
B likes A.
A likes X.
B doesn't like X.
What will be done to reduce the discomfort of being at odds with a friend?

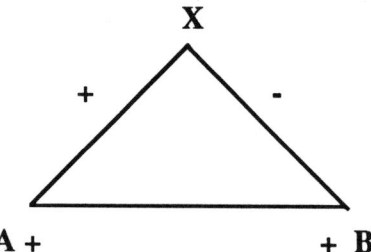

Fig. 5.2. Newcomb's balance theory. Source: Adapted from Theodore M. Newcomb. "An Approach to the Study of Communicative Acts." *Psychological Review* 60(1953):393-404.

1. After pondering the model, identify three situations in which you have seen evidence of a strain toward symmetry.

2. Attempt to identify situations in which the strain toward symmetry might not prevail, that is, when the strain toward symmetry might be overshadowed by other considerations.

MASS MEDIA MODEL

Perhaps the most widely used model of mass communication was offered by Westley and MacLean in the late 1950s. As does the Lasswell model, it seems simple now, almost self-evident. But at the time it represented important new knowledge. It helped us to conceptualize the process of mass communication and to focus our attention on specific parts of the process. See Figure 5.3.

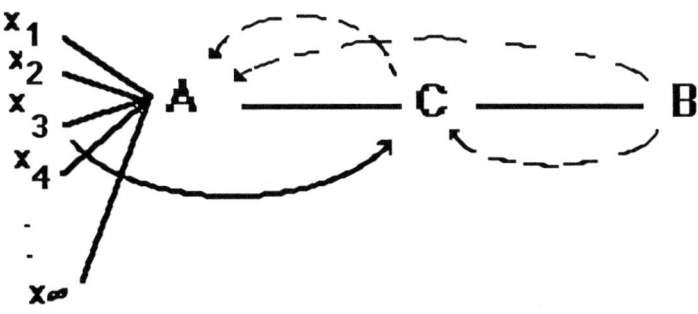

Fig. 5.3. The Westley-MacLean model of mass communication. Source: Bruce Westley and Malcolm MacLean, "A Conceptual Model for Communications Research," *Journalism Quarterly* 34(1957):31-83.

The Westley-MacLean model is described in detail in the suggested reading for this chapter. Most simply, the model can be considered an extension of the Newcomb ABX model but expanded from a two-person model to a mass communications model. The model suggests that person B receives stimuli/messages from communicator C about object X in the presence of person A. Let's say that C = a radio station, B = you, A = a friend or relative of yours, and X = an event or object. The point is that C has to select from the field of Xs, A may be either in the presence of C or B, B may communicate back to C or to A (feedback), and/or Xs may be perceived directly by C without intervention of A. After studying the model, answer the following questions.

1. Consider the Westley-MacLean model: Is any significant aspect of the process of mass communication omitted? Discuss.

2. Can you improve upon the model in any way? If you were building the model, would you add other elements? Discuss.

EXERCISE

To build your own model, you need to look broadly at your classroom communication situation. In your imagination, remove yourself to a far corner and observe the class. Who communicates with whom, how, when, etc.? Is there equal communication between all participants, or do some dominate? Is there feedback? Does communication follow a pattern?

As a simple exercise in model building, draw a model representing communication in this classroom. Include not only your role in the class but that of the professor and the entire class; signify one-way and interactive relationships.

UNIT 6

News Choices: Gatekeeping

READING:
James K. Buckalew. "News Elements and Selection by Television News Editors." *Journal of Broadcasting* 14(1969-70):47-54.

Paul B. Snider. "Mr. Gates Revisited: A 1966 Version of the 1949 Case Study." *Journalism Quarterly* 44(1967):419-27.

Gatekeeping is an important idea in communication theory and research. It was suggested by David Manning White in a study of an editor's news choices. The term suggests that a newsperson opens and closes the news "gates," letting some news go forward and stopping other items according to a mix of personal and professional preferences. This is important because a person's biases may lead to omission or inclusion of some items and because news selections color our "pictures" (our knowledge) of distant events. The following exercise illustrates news choices in one edition of the *New York Times*.

EXERCISE

Each of the headlines below appeared in the *NYT*. Some appeared on page 1, and others appeared elsewhere in the same edition. Read the entire list of headlines and draw an asterisk by each story you feel either was or should have been on page 1. Your instructor has the key to the actual story placements.

Be prepared to discuss the number of correct responses (agreement with the *NYT* as to which stories were on page 1) and to discuss your rationale for your own choices. It may be necessary for you to project yourself into the role of a *NYT* editor so that you can apply the judgments that support what you believe to be the policies of the *NYT*.

Selection of Headlines from One Edition of the *New York Times*

1. India's Spy Scare Slows Arms Deals
2. Wind and Cold Hit Wide Area of U.S.; Radio Programs Cut
3. Despair Wrenches Farmers' Lives as Debts Mount and Land Is Lost
4. China Assails U.S. on Population Funds
5. Report Puts Total of West Bank Settlers at 42,500
6. Jamaican Fire-brand Re-emerges with Old Spirit
7. Artificial Heart Works Well but Memory Fails

8. Duarte Denies U.S. Supports His Rivals
9. North Korea Offers to Return Two Captured Vessels to South
10. Kohl Gives the U.S. Guarded Support on Space Defense
11. U.S. Says Russians Try to Make Satellite of Central America
12. Soviet Ship Mutiny Chronicled
13. Iran Drops Oil Prices Closer to OPEC Levels
14. Dog Food Is Proposed with a Secret Ingredient: Birth Control
15. Computer-falsified Grades Raise New Issues at Colleges
16. N.Y. Post's Settlement Sets a Mark in Libel Suit
17. President's Record in Job Training Disputed
18. Judges Continuing to Uphold Quotas
19. Book on Illegal Dumping of Waste Protested by Congressman
20. Enrollment in Professional Schools Declining
21. Three Die in Rooming House Fire
22. Reagan Urges a Spirit of Cooperation on Budget
23. Mixup at U.S. Research Clinic Fatal to 20-Month-Old Boy
24. Nicaragua Says its Fiscal Shape Is "Hellish"

1. Discuss your rationale for deciding which stories would probably have been published on page 1. (That is, what qualities did you look for to decide whether a story warranted page 1 coverage?)

2. Does placement on page 1 give a story extra emphasis? In other words, suppose you read story 8 on page 15, but someone else read the same story on page 1; would your two evaluations of the importance of the story be the same? If not, what would make the difference? Discuss.

3. Examine your own list of page 1 stories; do you see any patterns? For example, did you select mostly national/international news? Much crime/violence news? Other conflict? News of politics? Were you motivated by (1) the need to sell newspapers, (2) the need to inform people of world events, (3) other needs? Discuss.

4. Were you, in effect, a gatekeeper? Were your judgments based solely on news and audience criteria, or did personal values slip quietly into some of your decisions? Discuss.

UNIT 7
Propaganda: Characteristics and Practice

READING:
Leonard I. Pearlin and Morris Rosenberg. "Propaganda Techniques in Institutional Advertising." *Public Opinion Quarterly* 16(1952)1: 5-26.

The term *propaganda* grew out of World War I and remained prominent on the research agenda through the next 30 to 40 years. The fact that propaganda is of greatest concern in time of war underscores its political implications. Lasswell identified the following major objectives of propaganda, which, as you will see, relate to war concerns:

1. Mobilize hatred against the enemy.
2. Preserve the friendship of allies.
3. Preserve friendship and secure cooperation of neutrals.
4. Demoralize the enemy.[1]

But is propaganda limited to the procurement or maintenance of political/military power? Let's examine some of the characteristics of propaganda.

1. Attempts to create or change opinions, attitudes, values.
2. Attempts to create or change toward a particular point of view.
3. Can be either covert or overt appeals.
4. Will be addressed to large-scale audience.
5. Will use mass media to spread message.

Is advertising a kind of propaganda? We think not, if the purpose of the advertising is to sell a product. If the purpose is to sell an idea or an image, it may be more nearly so. Propaganda, after all, is designed to win opinions.
Advertising aside, is international political propaganda a thing of the past? Can you identify instances of propaganda from any recent situation?

---

1. Harold Lasswell, *Propaganda Techniques in the World War* (New York: Peter Smith, 1927).

EXERCISES

Part A. Identify and be prepared to discuss in class: instances of propaganda by East or West in any recent wartime situation. (The East includes Russia, China, North Korea; the West includes the United States, England, France, West Germany.)

Identify and be prepared to discuss in class: instances of propaganda in any recent cold war situation at home or abroad. (A "cold war" is a war of nerves and threats, a time of chills in international relations.)

Part B. In a book called *The Fine Art of Propaganda*, Alfred McClung Lee and Elizabeth Briant Lee (1939) identified seven common "devices" of propaganda. These are given below. Are they relevant today? Read some newspapers and magazines, including their advertising, and watch television carefully; do not exclude radio. Try to find current examples of each of the devices. Identify the source of the device. For example, if the device was seen in *Newsweek*, write the name of the periodical and the page number, identify it as news copy or advertisement, and indicate date and page; explain carefully how it fits the propaganda device.

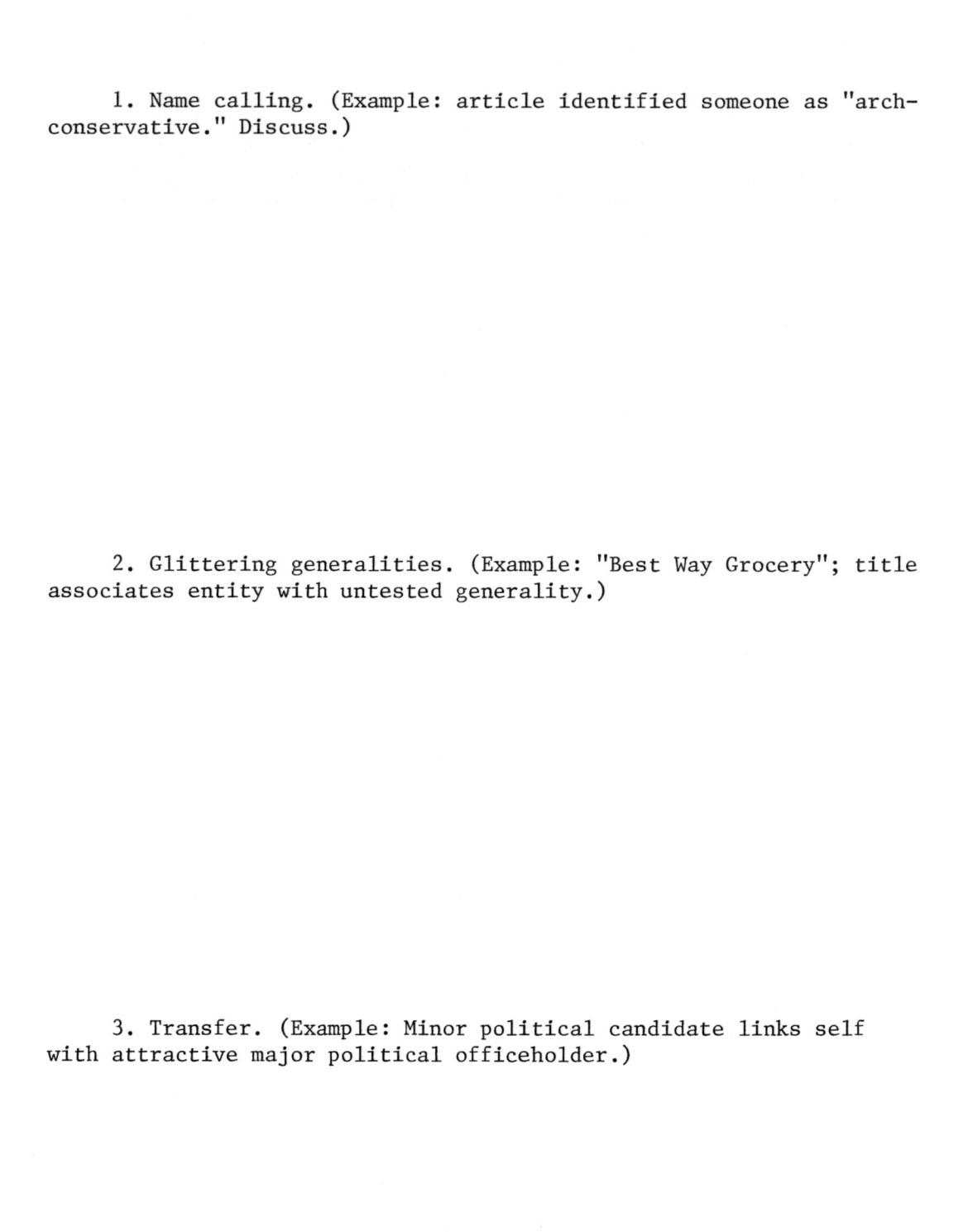

1. Name calling. (Example: article identified someone as "arch-conservative." Discuss.)

2. Glittering generalities. (Example: "Best Way Grocery"; title associates entity with untested generality.)

3. Transfer. (Example: Minor political candidate links self with attractive major political officeholder.)

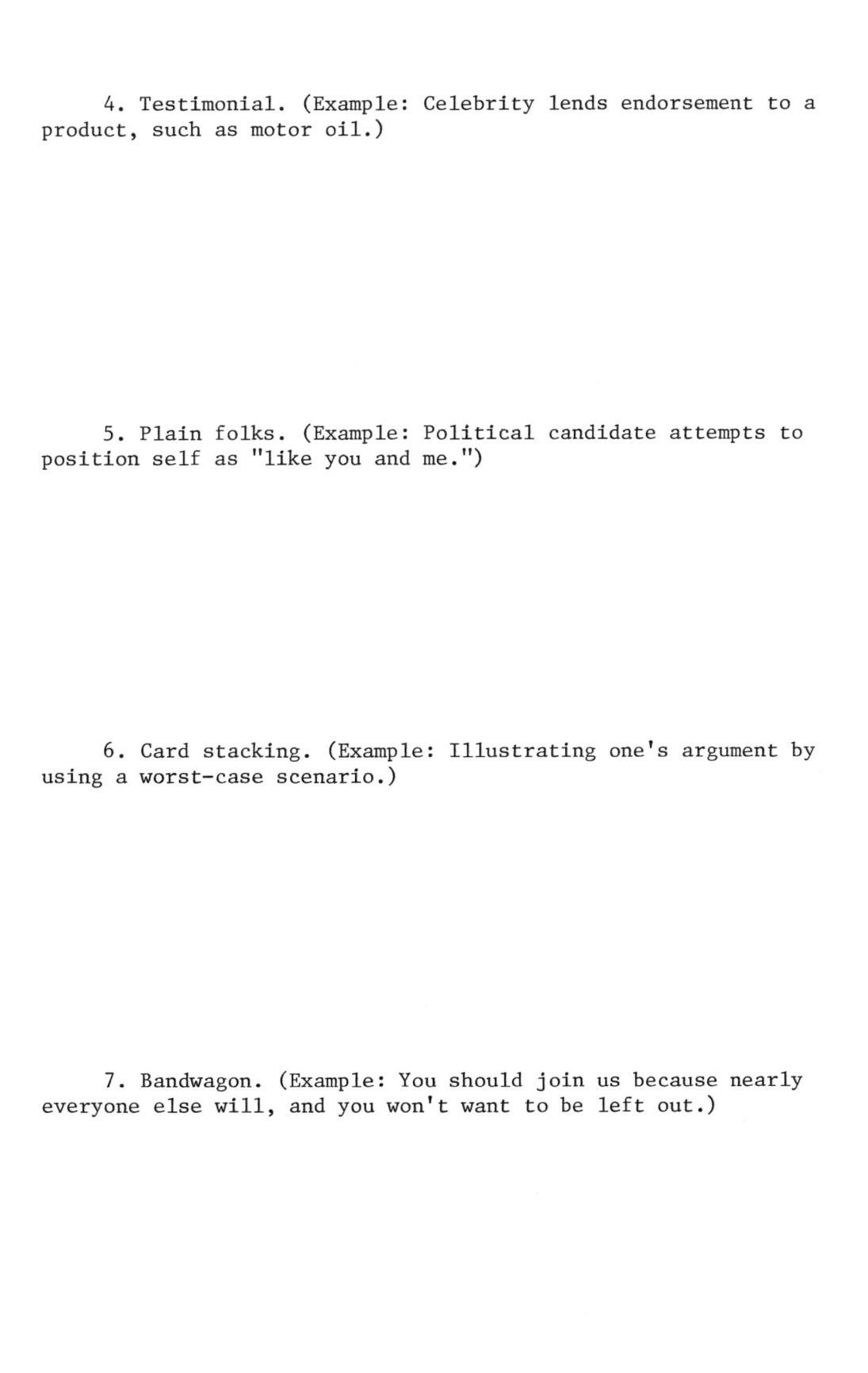

4. Testimonial. (Example: Celebrity lends endorsement to a product, such as motor oil.)

5. Plain folks. (Example: Political candidate attempts to position self as "like you and me.")

6. Card stacking. (Example: Illustrating one's argument by using a worst-case scenario.)

7. Bandwagon. (Example: You should join us because nearly everyone else will, and you won't want to be left out.)

Part C. Another persuasive device of which students of propaganda should be aware could be called "association," or even (in the vernacular) "good vibes." The technique is to link a product or an idea with another product or idea that is highly valued or warmly held. For example, we recall a commercial that said, "Purina dog chow. . . . All you add is love." The dog food, which had no intrinsic attractiveness, was linked with a warm feeling (love) and also implicitly with some cuddly pet. The authors recall seeing a 5-gallon can of heavy-duty floor cleaner. The can was not beautiful. But it was painted with bright colors, and it carried the picture of a beautiful woman in a bikini. Apparently, the attempt was to pair the product with a favorable attribute. We should hasten to add that there is nothing inherently sinister in these examples; the point is raised here only for purpose of awareness and thought.

Look about you in your media life and see if you can identify other associations or pairings that attempt to influence how we feel about an idea or product. Include newspaper, radio, television, or other advertising. List several instances. Provide sufficient source and content detail so that another person might be able to locate the same item. What is the pairing? The context? The purpose?

1.

2.

3.

UNIT 8

News Styles

READING:
Lewis Donohew. "Newswriting Styles: What Arouses the Reader?" *Newspaper Research Journal* 3(1982):3-6.

How a news story should be written has been the subject of concern and debate among news editors and reporters since the evolution of mass media. The earliest newspaper articles were laden with the writer's opinion, and this was considered normal for the time, perhaps through the penny press era of the mid-1800s.

With the coming of wire services, which provided war news to a variety of newspapers, newswriting styles changed to stress the news event and omit political opinion. The inverted pyramid style of presentation was developed to provide the most important facts at the beginning of the story. Giving the major facts first was crucial in case there was interference or a break in the telegraph transmission.

While the inverted pyramid writing style is still considered the industry standard for hard news, editors are more concerned today with reader appeal. How should the story be written so readers will understand? Which writing style will raise reader interest levels? Which styles are easiest to read, most enjoyable, most engaging?

The writing style debate continues today. Among styles being reevaluated are the traditional inverted pyramid and the narrative or "storytelling" approach, as well as variations of the two.

EXERCISE

Here is a story you should read and then answer the questions that follow:

FAIRBANKS--Four persons were killed and 12 were injured as a shooting incident between American Wilderness Organization (AWO) protesters and federal agents brought the "Pipeline Train" back to its berth here today.

Alaska Gov. Donald Weaks has ordered two rifle companies of national guardsmen to the tense scene in a clearing 20 miles south of Fairbanks where an estimated 5,000 AWO members and sympathizers have vowed to hold their ground following the short gun battle.

Solons who directed passage this summer of the bill to erect a huge pipeline from Alaska to Lincoln, Neb., left on schedule in a small touring train which was to follow the pipeline's route to Lincoln.

A crowd of some 5,000 had gathered during the week at Willis Creek Junction where the train was scheduled to make its first water stop. Leaders of the AWO had prepared a petition to read to congressmen on the train, protesting building the pipeline.

While the AWO talked with Sen. Adam Jennings, (D-Minn.), and other congressmen outside the train, angry shouts were heard from the crowd. Federal agents acting as bodyguards moved between the group at the train and the crowd, and seconds later gunfire was being exchanged between the agents and a few persons in the crowd while most tried to get out of the line of fire.

Congressmen were hurried back into the train

which left the scene. One federal agent, Adam G. Doget, 38, of Washington, was killed as were two men and a woman in the crowd. The injured were evacuated by helicopter in undetermined condition. Names of the victims were withheld pending notification of next of kin.

AWO leader Berry Waltson, who headed the petition contingency at the train, said after the event his group will remain in the clearing to prevent any further attempts at touring the pipeline throughway. "By opening fire on 5,000 unarmed people," Waltson said, the government has "proven its disregard for life."

He added the AWO members will "lie on the tracks if need be to show that the three innocent victims of today's massacre did not die in vain."

After leaving the train in Fairbanks, Sen. Jennings said he was "shocked to learn a band of criminals could waste the lives of innocent people just to gain public attention for a lost cause." He said he would press for an investigation of the incident to "bring the perpetrators to justice."

	Yes	No	Not Sure
1. Did you enjoy the story?	___	___	___
2. Did the story tell what happened?	___	___	___
3. Did you like the writing style?	___	___	___
4. Was it an honest account of what happened?	___	___	___
5. Did it answer all questions about events?	___	___	___
6. Was the length appropriate?	___	___	___
7. Would you have been satisfied with your work if you had written this story?	___	___	___
8. Do you think a newspaper would publish it?	___	___	___
9. Do you think a newspaper should publish it?	___	___	___

Now read story 2 and complete the questions that follow:

JUNEAU, Alaska--A predicted peaceful demonstration mushroomed into a national crisis this morning as gunshots erupted between federal marshals on the "Pipeline Train" and members of the American Wilderness Organization, (AWO), at a clearing 20 miles south of here.

Four persons, including a Secret Service bodyguard, were killed in the brief shooting battle. Twelve others were injured and evacuated by helicopter in undetermined condition.

Alaska Gov. Donald Weaks gave orders at 10 a.m. dispatching two rifle companies of national guardsmen who are due to arrive at the site before nightfall.

The Pipeline Train, carrying congressmen who directed the passage of legislation this summer approving a huge Alaska-Nebraska overland oil artery, departed Fairbanks at 8 a.m. for what was to be a five-day tour of the coming pipeline's route.

By mid-day yesterday, an estimated 5,000 persons--members of the American Wilderness Organization and sympathizers from across the country--were camped in the clearing near Willis Creek Junction waiting the small train's first water stop to make an official protest of the pipeline.

All was quiet as the medium-gauge rail line eased to a hissing halt below the water tower in the clearing. A committee of some half-dozen AWOs in jeans and T-shirts approached the passenger cars with a petition to read to the crowd of on-lookers and officials aboard the train.

Sen. Adam Jennings, (D-Minn.), led fellow congressmen and a handful of bodyguards out the train to await the AWO contingents. They met and were talking when rumblings began from the depths of the crowd. Shouts were heard and in the confusion Secret Service men moved between the crowd and the small group at the train, drawing their sidearms.

Mass confusion soon followed as shots popped off the side of the train, cracked into windows and tossed up little clouds of dust at the congressmen's feet. Agents' automatics were firing, barreling bullets into the crowd. Some youths were fleeing, most were lying on the ground while white puffs of smoke hung over the center of the throng.

Congressmen were shuffled unceremoniously back into the train as the agents shielded them. The whole incident, including screams, panic and death, lasted only half a minute.

AWO leader Berry Waltson, who headed the

petition assemblage at the train, said after the event his group would remain in the clearing to prevent any further attempts at touring the pipeline throughway.

"Our reasons for being here," Waltson said, "was only to tell the government we still opposed the pipeline. By opening fire on 5,000 unarmed people, they have proven their disregard for life."

He added the AWO members will "lie on the tracks if need be to prove Americans are still opposed to `big brother' government, and to show that the three innocent victims of today's massacre did not die in vain."

After debarking the train on its return trip to Juneau, Sen. Jennings said he was "shocked to learn a band of criminals could waste the lives of innocent people just to gain public attention for a lost cause. I intend to press for a full investigation of this tragic incident and bring the perpetrators to justice."

Killed at the clearing was agent Adam G. Doget, 38, of Washington, two young men and a young woman whose names are being withheld pending notification of their families. The condition of the injured was unavailable at noon.

The AWO had arranged the Alaskan clearing protest when it was announced last month congressmen would tour the length of the proposed oil line by train. Leaders have insisted it would be no more than an effort to make a vocal protest against possible damage to wildlife over the more than 3,5000-mile terrain.

	Yes	No	Not Sure
1. Did you enjoy the story?	___	___	___
2. Did the story tell what happened?	___	___	___
3. Did you like the writing style?	___	___	___
4. Was it an honest account of what happened?	___	___	___
5. Did it answer all questions about events?	___	___	___
6. Was the length appropriate?	___	___	___
7. Would you have been satisfied with your work if you had written this story?	___	___	___
8. Do you think a newspaper would publish it?	___	___	___
9. Do you think a newspaper should publish it?	___	___	___

Here is the final story to read and answer questions on:

ANCHORAGE--How can death be called ludicrous? Tragic, blasphemous, wretched, atrocious, abominable yes, but only under the most peculiar of circumstances could death ever be called ludicrous...and so was the title applied--earned--at Willis Creek Junction.

What brought us there? Street people, housewives, the young bearded blue-jeaned T-shirt sandals with a strap between the big and second toe idealist and his wife-women and toddler. Many coming four thousand miles (Oh, one and a half times across America, Jeeves) hitching rides from Illinois and California just to camp at a clearing and wait while a train takes on water for a petition to be read asking that an overland pipeline which will be constructed, not be constructed because of what it may do to the wilderness. That is ludicrous.

What brought us there was for most the numbers. If you believe strongly enough, you could take a week out of our life and be seen on television (or even not seen on television) when the numbers counted. You might bring a friend; camping out isn't so bad even in Alaska, and the cause is a good one. We had more than our share of the curious too, it is fair to add, the reporters and cameramen and the hot sandwich vending trucks that drove in from God knows where, perfect chrome-clad antitheses of buzzards over rotting flesh, but just as much scavengers. We were rather small and orderly group, letting our attention drift from someone's guitar strumming to the radio to helping erect a tent to just talking with one another, something that isn't done any more...do you remember the last time?

Just people. People who believed in America; maybe not as you see it today in Rockefeller Center looking up or on the strip in Las Vegas or in the pink brick and plastic suburbs outside St. Louis. These were peaceful people who

33

thought enough of the unspoiled ground to come to a clearing in the middle of nowhere and raise a last small cry for sanity.

But let's face it. Prior conduct is no indication of what may happen in a crisis, and, dear reader, when the train arrived, there was a crisis, the most ludicrous I've ever witnessed. When a huge jet plane falls from the sky...when it just begins plummeting down crazily wing over wing, tail over nose and you're sure the inevitable is approaching at thirty-two feet per second straight down, somehow (perhaps because our minds were not designed for realism on that magnitude) all we can do is laugh. Look! The impossible is happening! It's so ludicrous.

So it was as the little train pulled into the clearing and hssssssssssssed with that brass-wheels-on-iron-rails screech--to a stop under the water tower. Shades of my younger years; it was a scene right out of Saturday matinee at the Bijou. The train pulls into sight and screeches to a halt at the water tower in the clearing. All is quiet but the background music. Eyes are drawn to the platform between passenger cars. (Raise music to crescendo.) The brim of a black 10-gallon hat inches into view, then, there he is: Jack Palance with a moustache, black suit, silver studs, menacing esoteric sneer and long, thin cigar. He stands on the platform and glares at the peasants from above. Then his sidekicks appear: the Spanish American (we called them Mexicans then) with his crossed pistol belts, sombrero behind his head and gold teeth flashing in the sun; a scar-faced gunslinger; three nondescript extras in dirty vests; a riverboat gambler with pin-stripe suit and watch fob...and they all follow Palance onto the dust beside the train.

Enter stage left the guys in white hats. Not John Wayne but the milder variety Alan Ladd and Roy Rogers and their sidekicks Tonto and Pancho and a few friendly ranchers. They talk...and there is rumbling in the crowd...and (here's the most ludicrous part of all), they just start blam, blam, blam, blam, blam, blam, blam, blam, blasting away at the people in the crowd while people scream and run away and duck to the ground and die. Then the guys in black get back on the train and they ride into the sunset.

One of the guys in black is lying dead by the tracks; two young men and a young woman are dead in the crowd; and our wounded are crying. Half an hour later, helicopters come in and take them away. Ambulances and police cars arrive for the bodies and to "just keep an eye on things" with rifles and tear gas as they ring the campgrounds. We're told the national guard will be here soon to take everything in hand. I have a feeling, dear reader, things will not be in hand for a very long time.

	Yes	No	Not Sure
1. Did you enjoy the story?	___	___	___
2. Did the story tell what happened?	___	___	___
3. Did you like the writing style?	___	___	___
4. Was it an honest account of what happened?	___	___	___
5. Did it answer all questions about events?	___	___	___
6. Was the length appropriate?	___	___	___
7. Would you have been satisfied with your work if you had written this story?	___	___	___
8. Do you think a newspaper would publish it?	___	___	___
9. Do you think a newspaper should publish it?	___	___	___

After having read the three stories, can you select the author of each story from the photos in Figure 8.1?

Fig. 8.1. Can you select the authors of the three stories?

Now that you have completed the experimental procedures (please don't continue until you have), your instructor can take the class through a rating procedure with a show of hands on each of the nine points for the three stories. Since this is a straightforward rating comparison, the class should be able to suggest and decide an efficient way to tally the results in class, spending no more than 15 minutes arriving at a rough approximation of opinion on the three story types. While the class does its group rating, every individual should keep track of his or her own rating to determine how he or she has rated the three articles compared with how the class rates them.

This experiment is an attempt to study opinion about a style of writing that was gaining some attention (and great debate) in the early 1970s. Called "new journalism," the idea was that since reporters cannot be totally objective even if they strive to be, they should offer no pretenses. A more honest representation of events would be given if reporters let the reader know from which point of view they are writing. This is achieved by including such information in their stories. By this rationale the more politically controversial a story might be, the more necessary it is to emphasize the reporter's bias.

Without dwelling on this journalistic fad of the Vietnam War era, it is possible to treat the three stories as: story 1, a "straight" news story; story 2 a "color" news story; and story 3, a highly colorful news analysis written from a first-person perspective--not your average news story. The question then becomes, Are readers willing to accept the more colorful story treatments? The outcome, when this experiment was conducted for a group of high school juniors and seniors attending a summer journalism workshop, was that story 2 was a favorite, story 1 was acceptable, and story 3 was tripe (at best).[1]

How did your class analysis compare with that of the high school students done in the mid-1970s?

How did your personal appraisal of the stories compare with that of your class?

There is another aspect of this experiment that is tossed in and masked as well as possible. When you tried to match stories with pictures of the writers, you left the realm of writing style comparisons and entered the realm of stereotyping. Stereotypes are defined by Walter Lippmann in his 1921 work, *Public Opinion,* as "the pictures in our heads." Lippmann said that the news media provide, over time, information of the "hidden environment," or people, places, and events we can't experience firsthand. We rely on the news media, relatives, and friends to provide information, and we become libraries of stored pictures that allow us to deal with new information. When we hear the word "Russian," we have an image of what Russian means. If everyone in the class jots down half a dozen words that express "Russian," the

---

1. Gerald Stone, "'New Journalism' Finishes Poor Third in Syracuse Study," *Journalism Educator* 31(1976):45-48.

chances are there will be a lot of overlap among the lists so created--less so if the class is composed of international students whose background is likely to differ substantially, hence whose stereotype of "Russian" would also differ.

Now consider this. If you rated one of the three stories as likeable, honest, and publishable, what criteria did you use to determine which of the nine authors wrote it? What about the story you didn't like? What criteria did you use to determine that author? Did your own stereotypes about writers, males and females, race, age, and dress have much to do with your decision? If you didn't apply your own preconceptions of people, based on your regard for the three stories, how did you decide who the authors were?

By the way, none of the people in the pictures wrote any of the articles. You could have been asked simply to select which person was Jewish, Catholic, or Protestant (experiments have been done matching pictures with preconceptions of people's religion), but the intent of the selection (the purpose of the experiment) would have been too obvious. The experiment would not have been well masked.

UNIT 9
Bias and Stereotypical Portrayals

READING:
Fred Fedler, Mike Meeske, and Joe Hall. "*Time* Magazine Revisited: Presidential Stereotypes Persist." *Journalism Quarterly* 56(1979): 353-59.

John C. Merrill. "How *Time* Stereotyped Three U.S. Presidents." *Journalism Quarterly* 42(1965):563-70.

Some years ago when John C. Merrill (then at the University of Missouri) conducted a study of *Time*, he showed that what nearly everyone recognized as a lively style of writing also masked an element of political bias. The magazine had a way of throwing in occasional words that, in an otherwise unobjectionable piece, might subtly build a positive or negative image. Recent research indicates that the bias might still be found. This line of research is interesting for a couple of reasons. It gives us the opportunity to critique a popular research method, and it focuses our attention on the nature of bias.

Merrill relied on a form of content analysis. He chose 10 editions from *Time* during the administrations of presidents Truman, Eisenhower, and Kennedy. (Unfortunately, he did not select corresponding periods for each administration for more relevant comparison.) In those editions, he focused on the language used to describe the behavior of each president. He was especially interested in the presence or absence of loaded words and in general contextual impressions. Merrill identified six categories of *bias*.

    1. *Attribution bias* stems from the magazine's attribution of information to the president, such as bias contained in synonyms for "said." Example: if the magazine states that the president "snapped" rather than "said."
    2. *Adjective bias* involves words that describe a person. Examples: the "brooding" president, in a "serene" state of mind, using a "flat, monotonous voice."
    3. *Adverbial bias* relies on qualifiers to make a point. Example: the president "barked sarcastically." Such adverbs are subjective, the opinion of the writer.
    4. *Contextual bias* is the result of the whole story.
    5. *Outright opinion* is expressed in direct statements of support or opposition.
    6. *Photographic bias* can be seen in positive or negative impressions of the person created through publication of photographs. Example: picture of a president licking his lips or in an awkward fall.

EXERCISE

Armed with these categories of bias, we can attempt to replicate the Merrill study. This exercise will illustrate some of the difficulties of research as well as, perhaps, the subtleties of bias. Merrill used only *Time*; your instructor may wish to consider using both *Time* and *Newsweek*. Use the following procedure (modifying instructions as needed):

1. The instructor or an assistant should coordinate the exercise.
2. Each student should be assigned to an edition of a newsmagazine.
3. Half the class should work with *Newsweek* and half work with *Time*.
4. Select one week with which to begin the examination; use this for each magazine and each presidential administration.
5. The number of editions examined should depend on the number of students in the class; a large sample is desirable.
6. Identify stories that are to be examined; include any story whose primary intent is reportage or analysis on the president or his administration. Use news columns, not syndicated columns.
7. Ignore contextual bias, since it may be too vague and too subjective to be useful.
8. Ask student coders (members of the class) to examine each word and photograph in light of Merrill's categories and to make note of each instance of apparent bias.
9. On an assigned date, tabulate data in class.

While Merrill studied Truman, Eisenhower, and Kennedy, we will examine references to Nixon, Ford, Carter, and Reagan.

Dates: President Reagan, 1980+   President Ford, 1974-76
       President Carter, 1976-80   President Nixon, 1968-74

Suggestion: Study editions of the July to December months in the first year of each presidency. This will get you past the "honeymoon" period. If not every edition can be studied, select each nth edition. For example, student 1 examines the first edition in July; student 2 the 3rd edition, etc. Read and code all stories whose focus is on administration news.

Data may be displayed as in Table 9.1. This design will give an indication of whether the magazines treated each president similarly or whether treatment varied. But we should note that there is no particular reason to expect treatment to be identical; some presidents probably are "better" than others. If a president is described as "snapping" or "brooding" or as "bellowing" the description is not necessarily biased; it may be accurate. That is why we suggest using two or more newsmagazines; we can compare one with another.

Table 9.1. How to Display Attribution Bias

	Time		*Newsweek*	
	Favorable	Unfavorable	Favorable	Unfavorable
Nixon	frequency = 14 percent = 15%	7 7%		
Ford	32 34%	10 11%		
Carter	15 16%	15 16%		
Reagan				

All students participating in this exercise should use the same coding form. The coding form (sample form given below) should show (1) the name of the publication, (2) the edition from which the data are taken, (3) the page number(s) from which the data are taken, (4) the example of bias, (5) the judgment as to whether the word or phrase is positive or negative (favorable or unfavorable), and (6) the name or initials of the coder. Such information will be useful in class discussions and in estimating research reliability. (Reliability refers to the reproducibility of the results.)

Read each word of selected stories (political stories dealing with a presidential administration). Examine adjectives and adverbs for probable bias. List each word you consider loaded in either the favorable or the unfavorable column. By "loaded" we mean any word that has nonobjective meaning.

CODING FORM

Name of Newsmagazine_____ Date_____ Page_____

President_____ Coder_____

Attribution Bias

Favorable		Unfavorable	
1.	9.	1.	9.
2.	10.	2.	10.
3.	11.	3.	11.
4.	12.	4.	12.
5.	13.	5.	13.
6.	14.	6.	14.
7.	15.	7.	15.
8.	16.	8.	16.

Adjective Bias

Favorable		Unfavorable	
1.	9.	1.	9.
2.	10.	2.	10.
3.	11.	3.	11.
4.	12.	4.	12.
5.	13.	5.	13.
6.	14.	6.	14.
7.	15.	7.	15.
8.	16.	8.	16.

Adverbial Bias

Favorable		Unfavorable	
1.	9.	1.	9.
2.	10.	2.	10.
3.	11.	3.	11.
4.	12.	4.	12.
5.	13.	5.	13.
6.	14.	6.	14.
7.	15.	7.	15.
8.	16.	8.	16.

Contextual Bias

Favorable		Unfavorable	
1.	9.	1.	9.
2.	10.	2.	10.
3.	11.	3.	11.
4.	12.	4.	12.
5.	13.	5.	13.
6.	14.	6.	14.
7.	15.	7.	15.
8.	16.	8.	16.

Outright Opinion		Photographic Bias	
Favorable[a]	Unfavorable[b]	Favorable[c]	Unfavorable
1.	1.	1.	1.
2.	2.	2.	2.
3.	3.	3.	3.
4.	4.	4.	4.
5.	5.	5.	5.
6.	6.	6.	6.
7.	7.	7.	7.
8.	8.	8.	8.
9.	9.	9.	9.

Examples: [a] = president shaking hands, smiling, AOK.
[b] = president falling (tripping) over a TV cable; looks clumsy.
[c] = president described as "doing a terrific job," etc.

UNIT 10

The Knowledge Gap

READING:
Cecille Gaziano. "The Knowledge Gap: An Analytical Review of Media Effects." *Communication Research* 10(1983):447-86.

Phillip J. Tichenor, George A. Donohue, and Clarice N. Olien. "Mass Media Flow and Differential Growth in Knowledge." *Public Opinion Quarterly* 34(1970):159-70.

Before reading the material on the following pages, complete the inventory below:

1. What was your grade average in grades 5 through 9? If you do not recall, choose a response that indicates your best estimate.

    1.5   2.0   2.5   3.0   3.5   4.0

2. About how much time per day on weekdays (on average) did you spend doing homework when you were in grades 5 through 9? If you do not remember precisely, make your best estimate.

    ____less than 30 minutes   ____between 1 and 2 hours

    ____30 minutes to 1 hour   ____more than 2 hours

3. About how much did you enjoy school in grades 5 through 9?

    very much /___/___/___/___/___/ very little

4. Do you think your study habits in grades 5 through 9 have influenced your school grades since that time?

    ____yes ___no ___not sure

5. What was your approximate grade average in grades 10 through 12?

    1.5   2.0   2.5   3.0   3.5   4.0

6. What is or was your approximate grade point average as an undergraduate?

    1.5   2.0   2.5   3.0   3.5   4.0

7. Which of the following did your father complete?

___high school   ___4-year college graduate

___some college   ___at least some postgraduate work

8. Did your family own a set of encyclopedia when you were in grade school?

___yes   ___no

9. If yes, how frequently did you use the encyclopedia?

very frequently /___/___/___/___/___/ very infrequently

10. How often did you use your public library when you were in grades 5 through 9?

very frequently /___/___/___/___/___/ very infrequently

If you grew up in a home without a set of encyclopedia, you might have felt a little disadvantaged when a grade-school teacher assigned a weekend report that required one. You might have noticed that some members of class could do their work at home, while you or others had to go to a public library or to a friend's home.

The knowledge-gap hypothesis suggests, for example, that people who had easy access to an encyclopedia during grade school should have gained some educational advantage. That is, access to the encyclopedia should have provided some information gain or, at the least, some familiarity with the use of reference books.

Let's consider the questionnaire at the beginning of this unit and touch on the main aspects of the knowledge-gap hypothesis.

Looking back to grade 5, would you suppose that all the members of your class were similar in socioeconomic status? Did all the parents have similar educational experience and occupations? Most likely the answer to these questions is "no," and that is important because parents' occupation and income can have a bearing on a student's learning environment. Occupation is related to income, and income is related to certain educational advantages such as ownership of expensive reference volumes (encyclopedia). This isn't to say that merely owning an encyclopedia or other reference volumes is sufficient to enhance a student's position. A family might well have a fine set of books but never use them and may not in general have a favorable learning environment.

EXERCISE

Divide your class into groups based on educational level of fathers. Let's say that completion of high school, for our purposes, is "low educational achievement," although we hasten to acknowledge that many persons of modest formal education are extremely knowledgeable. And we will say that education beyond the baccalaureate degree is "high educational achievement." (If you wish, you could consider high school and some college as "low educational achievement," while college degree and some postbaccalaureate is "high educational achievement.") Our assumption is that education is related to ownership of an encyclopedia. We can illustrate the idea in a contingency table (Table 10.1), although we must emphasize that the numbers are fictional. If the instructor and students wish, actual frequencies from questions 7 and 8 of the questionnaire might be tallied and entered in a contingency table on the blackboard, using Table 10.1 as a guide.

Table 10.1. Father's Educational Level and Encyclopedia Ownership

	Owns Encyclopedia	Does Not Own Encyclopedia
Father: Low Educational Achievement	6	24
Father: High Educational Achievement	20	10

What is your own experience? Where are you in the contingency table? If your family owned an encyclopedia, was your father well educated? Do you think the suggested relationship between education and learning resources would hold for most cases, if not all?

Let's look at another possible relationship, that between your school grades and the availability of learning resources. First, take the average of your school grades from questions 1, 5, and 6. Now, refer to Table 10.1; put your average grade in the same cell where your own experience is represented. (Example: If your father was well educated and your family owned an encyclopedia, you are in the lower left cell; put your grade point average there too.) Chances are, although it won't necessarily be so, that grades are related to father's occupation and the availability of learning resources.

As stated above, merely having an encyclopedia is not enough; it must be used if it is to influence knowledge level. So let's expand Table 10.1 to include a measure of use. Referring to question 9, if you checked either of the two blanks on the left-hand end of the scale, you can be categorized as a "user" (encyclopedia user, that is). If you checked either of the two blanks on the right-hand end of the scale, you can be categorized as a "nonuser." The middle blank is "undecided" and can't be used here. In Table 10.2, we will enter some more fictional data to illustrate the direction we could predict actual data would go. For comparison, where would you fit into the table? Would your position in the table be consistent with the theory being discussed here? Would most people follow the suggested pattern?

Table 10.2. Education, Ownership of Learning Resource, and Use of Resource

Father's Education	Encyclopedia Owned — Used	Owned — Not Used	Not Owned
High School	7	7	16
College	18	4	5

Knowledge-gap theory is not yet able to predict precisely the outcomes attributable to access to learning resources, including mass media. Presumably, access has an impact on knowledge level if access results in use. In the case of the encyclopedia, its presence in your home may have had no impact on, say, your grades, but perhaps it contributed to your enjoyment of school. (As a test, you might enter your score for question 3 beside your grade point average in Table 10.1. Presumably, grades and enjoyment of school are also related.)

Consider two other variables: use of a library and amount of time spent with homework. Try placing your score on questions 2 and 10 in Table 10.1 in place of grade point or enjoyment. Are the numbers consistent? Theory would suggest that there will be a positive relationship among all four variables: grades, enjoyment, homework time, and use of a library. The whole idea of the theory focuses more on the idea of "appreciation for education" than on any single variable.

What are some counterpoints to the relationships we have suggested? In the first place, the class for which you do this exercise probably is not representative of the population at large. The fact that you and your colleagues are in college tends to truncate the range of grades, fathers' education, and the like, i.e., virtually all the relevant variables.

Having an encyclopedia in the home may not be a good predictor of later high school performance because parents might have made a conscious decision not to purchase an encyclopedia; they may have preferred that their children learn to use the library, certainly an important skill.

Finally, higher grades, more library use, more time with homework, and more use of the library may have more than one explanation, not just the availability of reference volumes. Performance depends on motivation, behavior models, environment, native ability, etc.

In general, the knowledge gap suggests that knowledge levels vary in relation to available resources, including media; but clearly, there are many factors to be accounted for. Improvements in communications technology could have the effect of increasing the knowledge gap if only a few have access or reducing the gap if access is widespread. We can watch with interest as research data accumulate.

UNIT 11
Theory of Relative Constancy

READING:
Maxwell E. McCombs. "Mass Media in the Marketplace." *Journalism Monographs* no. 24 (August 1972).

The theory of relative constancy is not one of the broad communication theories but is one of the few (and one of the earliest) theories on the topic of emerging new media technology.

In developing the theory, McCombs and Howard Scripps engaged in a massive investigation of marketing data collected nationwide over a period of some two decades. Their findings suggest several implications about how mass media audiences use the various media and predictions about how their allegiances might change with the emergence of new media into the marketplace. Here are several of the broad implications of the theory:

1. There is a constant percentage of the gross national product (GNP) that will be devoted to mass media use. If we say, for instance, that 3% of the GNP will be related to mass media expenses, we should not expect the percentage to change drastically from one year to the next.

2. Just as there is a fixed percentage of the GNP going to mass media on a national basis, a family's budget percentage that goes to mass media is also fixed. If a family is accustomed to spending 5% of its annual income on the mass media (goes to one movie a week, buys a newspaper subscription, replaces a television set every four years, has three magazine subscriptions, buys a new stereo, etc.), that percent of the family budget is unlikely to change drastically from year to year.

3. However, although the percentage for both the GNP and family expenses on mass media is constant, the actual dollars spent are not. As GNP increases in good years, the 3% related to mass media may mean that $100 billion is being spent on the media; in bad years, the 3% may mean that only $65 billion is being spent. The same is true for family media expenditures. As salaries and family income rise, the 3% may increase from $1,000 a year to $1,500 a year going to mass media; if there is a financial setback in the family, spending on the media will also be cut proportionately.

So although the percentage being spent is constant, the dollar amount is relative. The dollars spent will fluctuate depending on how many dollars there are to spend both on a national and an individual basis.

4. Since the percentage spent on mass media is constant, a new medium entering the marketplace results in the dollars going to all existing media being divided more thinly so that some dollars will be left for the new medium. When a new medium enters the marketplace, it doesn't draw a greater percentage of dollars toward the mass media. Instead, the existing media expense pie is merely subdivided into more pieces.

We may say that the new kid on the block is going to earn a place at the expense of all the others. The comparison is not like a baby being born to a family because in that case the family's food budget has to increase and take a larger percentage of the entire family budget; every member of the family has to eat. Instead, the analogy is more like the family's clothing budget. When there is a new child needing Dr. Denton's, it is likely that an older sibling will wait awhile for a new pair of shoes.

5. Emerging new media may be predicted to divide the income going to all existing media, but the new medium will have its greatest impact on the existing media whose properties it most closely matches. Hence a new broadcast medium is likely to draw more audience and resources away from existing broadcast media than from existing print media, and the medium whose best qualities are being duplicated or improved by the new medium will suffer most.

What happened when television became a pervasive home entertainment medium? The numbers of people attending movies decreased. Television is moving pictures with sound, very similar to movies, but has the advantage of being in the home and available much of the day. The theory of relative constancy suggests that the advent of television would have its greatest effect on the existing film and radio audiences (the electronic media), with its single greatest impact on movies.

6. As mass media proliferate, finances to support the new media may not be the most significant limiting factor that must be dealt with: time may constrict the new media more than finances. The idea here is that people's use of the mass media is already so great, there aren't enough hours in the day to devote more time to them. Most studies of how people spend their time indicate mass media use is only surpassed by the hours a day that people sleep or work. In a week's time, mass media use is by far the number one leisure activity of most Americans. If the average person is currently spending five to six hours a day with the mass media (some three hours with television; an hour with radio; more than half an hour with newspapers; some time with magazines, books, and an occasional movie; and not counting telephone time) we must predict that available time will be a major factor in a new medium's quest for its share of the marketplace.

Time, unlike money, is a finite commodity. There are only 24 hours in a day, and if the average adult spends eight hours sleeping, eight hours at work, one hour in transit, and two or more hours eating, that leaves only about five hours, most of which are already being spent with the media. Since no more hours can be added to the day, the addition of a new medium will mean audiences will have to greatly reduce or stop using one or more of the existing media. Instead of sharing the existing resources, the theory suggests, time restraints will force media into a struggle for survival.

EXERCISE

Part A. This exercise requires use of the precepts of the theory of relative constancy to predict what is happening and may continue to happen as cable television becomes more pervasive in the American media marketplace. Use the information on relative constancy to answer the following questions about cable TV.

1. From the list of existing mass media below, determine which is most likely to be adversely affected by the advent of cable TV. List the three media you think are most affected by cable, with "a" being the one most affected, then briefly explain why those choices were made.

    ___magazines   ___radio   ___records

    ___television   ___movies   ___books

    ___newspapers   ___telephone   ___home computers

a.

b.

c.

2. One significant effect of cable's spread has already been hinted at and in fact documented since the early 1980s. It is (not surprisingly) an aspect of television that was a dominating influence on the medium prior to the advent of cable, that is, the network system. Using the theory of relative constancy, explain how cable has affected network television.

3. Cable television can cost from about $10 per month to as much as $50 per month depending on where the individual family lives and the services subscribed to. When families get cable, they are committing themselves to an additional $120 to $600 a year in new mass media costs. Using the theory of relative constancy, how might the family's mass media purchases be altered when cable (and its costs) comes into the home?

4. What are existing media doing to improve their chances for survival and possible growth in light of cable TV's spread? Consider briefly each of the following existing media:

    a. Magazines:

    b. Records:

    c. Movies:

    d. Newspapers:

    Part B. As an alternate exercise, or in addition, change the emerging new medium from cable TV to home computers or to any appropriate item. Home computers may be the first new mass medium for which the theory of relative constancy does not apply because the near future of home computers is likely to include nontraditional applications. For instance, instead of being just an entertainment/information medium, home computers may usurp much of the family banking chore. Rather than going through the monthly routine of writing checks, addressing envelopes, mailing checks, and trying to balance the checkbook, all these activities may be done on the home computer. What are the implications of a mass medium being more than an entertainment/information device? What are some of the nontraditional applications other than banking that might be associated with pervasive use of home computers? Which of the existing mass media will be most adversely affected?

Optional: At the instructor's discretion, write a paper on the impact of home computers on the mass media marketplace.

UNIT 12
Attitudes and Attitude Change

READING:
Daniel Katz. "The Functional Approach to the Study of Attitudes." *Public Opinion Quarterly* 24(1960):163-204

Attitude is probably the most studied concept in social research. A computer search of the literature with just the keyword "attitude(s)" would yield thousands of articles. And attitudes are clearly a powerful force in human behavior, often determining a priori whether we accept or reject, believe or disbelieve. The branches of attitude research are too numerous to recount here. We will address only in broad strokes (1) the nature of attitudes and (2) the nature of attitude change.

ATTITUDES

Attitude has been defined as "an enduring system of positive or negative evaluations, emotional feelings, and pro and con action tendencies with respect to a social object."[1] Consider each of the words in the definition. Attitudes are enduring, not ephemeral; they are resistant to change. Attitudes are systematic, a kind of logical synthesis;[2] attitudes are the expression of cumulated thoughts, beliefs, and experiences. One might think of an attitude as a building whose structure is a mix of fact and feeling. Presumably, knowledge of the structure would allow prediction of an attitude.

Attitudes involve evaluations, which psychologists call affect; evaluations are a continuum that runs from positive to negative. Most simply, attitudes involve liking and disliking, approach-avoidance, and reward-reinforcement; attitudes are feelings. Attitudes have implications for behavior. We cannot say attitudes cause behavior, because sometimes (perhaps often) an attitudinal inclination is overridden by some other factor. For example, you may oppose (have negative attitude toward) something said in class, but your concern for peer approval may make it impossible for you to speak out. Hence, had we predicted your behavior based on your attitude, we might have been

---

1. D. Krech, R. S. Crutchfield, and E. L. Ballachey, *Individual in Society: A Textbook of Social Psychology* (New York: McGraw-Hill, 1962).
2. E. E. Jones and H. B. Gerard, *Foundations of Social Psychology* (New York: Wiley, 1967).

mistaken.[3] There are numerous examples in the literature in which attitudes as measures in research were inconsistent with subsequent behavior.

In fact, the measurement of attitudes is highly problematical. Often a person's thoughts on an issue are not well organized, so articulation of feeling is poor. Then again, the person may have thought out the issue, but may be unwilling to make any kind of overt declaration. To get around the problem, researchers usually rely on an index instead of a single attitude question. An index is a set of measures. So instead of asking one question such as "What is your attitude toward . . . ?" we may ask several different but related questions. In index form, attitude would be indicated by the sum of responses to the set of measures (or perhaps the mean of responses).

ATTITUDE CHANGE

If attitudes are learned (the cumulation of thoughts and experiences) and if they are generally resistant to change, what is the communicator to do? Is there no way to change an attitude once held? Does persuasion merely reinforce the strength of the listener's predisposition? Suppose it was your job to convince a large population that a previously unsavory practice was now acceptable; how would you proceed?

While we will not attempt a review of the literature, we can say that there are two models of persuasion whose elements should be examined. McGuire's model identified five steps that must be followed if persuasion is to occur.[4]

1. You must win the attention of the listener. Advertisers, among others, are familiar with attention-getting techniques.
2. If communication is to be effective, it must be comprehended. As a communicator, you may have a beautiful presentation; but if the message is garbled, the effect may be lost.
3. The listener must yield to the idea being presented. That is, if the listener rejects your information as useless, untrue, or whatever, your battle is lost. The listener must yield if persuasion is to occur.
4. The listener must retain your communication long enough to act upon it. If the listener pays scant attention and fails to retain your information, persuasion is likely to be lost.
5. A measure of your success is whether the listener is motivated to action.

---

3. Katz, "Functional Approach," pp. 163-76.
4. W. McGuire, "The Nature of Attitude Change," in G. Lindzey and E. Aronson, eds., *The Handbook of Social Psychology*, 2d ed., vol. 3 (Reading, Mass.: Addison-Wesley, 1969), pp. 136-314.

But McGuire said these factors did not act alone in successful persuasion; rather, persuasion further depends on source, message, channel, and receiver factors.

1. Consider the source of the communication. The persuader may win the listener's attention yet be unpersuasive due to any of several reasons, for example, bias, personal characteristics, semantic noise, etc. Attention is necessary but not sufficient.
2. Consider the message; it may interact with either of the steps in persuasion. For example, a message that gets the attention of the listener may be comprehensible but too complex to retain in sufficient detail for action.
3. Consider the channel; persuasion may depend on how the message is transmitted. A brochure may be effective in one case, while a film might be more effective in another.
4. Consider receiver characteristics. Education, experience, and personality all have a bearing on successful communication.

Fishbein and Ajzen proposed a more direct approach.[5] In their conception, attitudes are a function of a person's beliefs (cognitions) about an attitude object. An attitude creates *behavioral intentions* toward the object, and if the intention is not defeated by some other factor, it may lead to overt behavior toward the object. For example, to change an attitude, you must change the person's beliefs about the object. That sets it up clearly; the goal of persuasive communication would be to change the person's cognitions or beliefs about X. How to go about that? Intuition helps, but perhaps the communicator should address each of the source-audience factors mentioned above.

The student should be aware that our brief discussion here barely touches the surface of this area of research. There is much literature on communication sources (credibility, ethos), message structure, media, learning, inoculation, rehearsal, audience position, level of action, etc. Attitude study remains today a fruitful and intriguing field of research.

EXERCISES

Part A. Here you will analyze an attitude, so first identify an *attitude object*. An attitude object is anything about which you have an attitude. The object might be a person (such as a politician) or an issue (such as the Statue of Liberty). As a warm-up, let's say you selected "a college education" as your attitude object. You may have

---

5. M. Fishbein and I. Ajzen, *Belief, Attitude, Intention and Behavior: An Introduction to Theory and Research* (Reading, Mass.: Addison-Wesley, 1975).

strong positive feelings for a college education. Of course, not everyone shares your view; some people think education undesirable. If two people think differently about the same topic, how did they acquire their feelings? What kinds of thoughts, experience, or knowledge led you to assess a college education as having positive effects? Presumably, an attitude is the synthesis of a person's beliefs or knowledge about the issue.

On the College Education Pro-Con List that follows, check each statement with which you generally agree. Do that now.

COLLEGE EDUCATION PRO-CON LIST

Pro:
___Income increases with increases in education.
___Educated persons feel more in control of their life.
___Education leads to professionalism, an important goal.
___The more education you have, the more people respect you.
___Learning is among the highest goals of living.
___Educated persons are better citizens.
___Education leads to greater appreciation of the finer things life has to offer.
___Education leads to greater self-respect.
___Education opens doors that would be closed otherwise.
___Everyone, whether consciously or unconsciously, wants more education.

Con:
___A college education doesn't guarantee a good job.
___Beginning and early-year salaries don't warrant the expense and time of going to college.
___When all is said and done, there is little to learn in college.
___If teachers know so much, why aren't they rich?
___Those who can, do; those who can't, teach.
___There is no substitute for good, common sense.
___At least some of what you take in college is a waste of time.
___There are a lot of people in college today who shouldn't be in college at all.
___A person would be better off by spending two hours a day in a library instead of going to college for four years.
___Success in college has little relation to success in life.

The list represents a scale of your attitude about a college education's value. Add the number of check marks you made on the 10 positive statements; then add those on the 10 negative statements. Subtract the negative from the positive and consider your score a rating of your attitude intensity toward a college education. (A negative attitude is possible.)

The scale is an indication of the beliefs that lead to an attitude. We have the direction of the attitude and the intensity. But still we don't know whether or to what extent the attitude will affect behavior; we don't know your behavioral intentions. We could ask, "If you feel strongly that academic achievement is desirable, do you intend to complete your education?" And you probably would answer, "Yes." If your attitude was strong enough, you probably would complete your education, as you indicated. But if your attitude was slightly uncertain, then there would be a decreasing likelihood that you would complete your education.

And so you see the line of thought. Now select another attitude object and go through this process on your own. Make note of your thoughts and decisions as you go along, and in a paragraph below, summarize your feeling as to whether or not you actually have "analyzed" an attitude.

Part B. Suppose you are the company expert on communications. And the boss says to you, "Smidley, we need an information campaign that will convince the public our company puts public interest above profit. I'm sure you can do it." Armed with the discussion carried on in this exercise, devise a communications scenario that would help to save your job by winning the hearts of the public. Don't write a book; a paragraph or two will do.

PART TWO

Selected Theories and Hypotheses

UNIT 13
The Rise and Fall of Communication Theories

READING:
Elizabeth Noelle-Neumann. "Return to the Concept of Powerful Mass Media." In H. Eguchi and K. Sorta, eds., *Studies of Broadcasting: An International Annual of Broadcasting Science*. Tokyo: Nippoa Hoso Kyokai, 1973), pp. 67-112.

Despite popular sentiment of the type that says "the idea sounds great in theory, but what about in real life?" theory is not a four-letter word. Theory is to be valued and pursued. Theory is the stuff of which certainty is built. Theory allows us to predict relationships among variables. For example, we might predict that if A and B occur, then C is likely to follow. If our theories are supported by credible evidence, our knowledge of the relationships between variables can improve efficiency of communication behavior.

Novice students of communication theory often are somewhat exasperated by the dearth (if not absence) of rock-solid theories in their field and also by the tendency of communication theories to rise and fall. And one can appreciate their incredulity. How can an idea that seemed so certain yesterday, and on which presumably acceptable decisions were made, be so discredited today?[1] The literature of the field reveals several intriguing theoretical propositions that were researched enthusiastically but ultimately died on the vine.

For most of their history, the media were believed to be very powerful in their ability to motivate and influence people. Latter-day researchers called this pervasive belief the "bullet theory." The expression implied that media messages went directly from the medium to the receiver. And there was evidence to support the bullet theory; propaganda successes of World War I were fresh in the minds of consumers in the 1920s and 1930s.

But in the 1940s there was persuasive research (Lazarfeld's Ohio, New York, and New Jersey studies) to suggest that the media were only indirectly powerful and that the real communication power lay with "opinion leaders." And so the bullet theory was put aside and a new period of "limited effects research" began.

---

1. A similar point was suggested by Alexis Tan in *Mass Communication Theories and Research* (Columbus, Ohio: Grid, 1981), p. 5.

Over the period from the 1940s until the mid-1960s, the limited-effects tradition prevailed. But it became increasingly clear that the opinion leadership approach would not be useful. There were too many leaders; nearly everyone was an opinion leader for someone. The idea collapsed of its own weight.

The 1960s, a period of turmoil in which the media were accused of bearing bad news, saw the beginning of the return to the model of powerful media. It seemed clear, after all, that media did speak directly to many people and that some of them, at least, were influenced and motivated to act. So rather than refer naively to media as powerful, we preferred to speak of media as moderately powerful; we recognized that if the media said, "Vote for Smith," some would and some would not. We recognized that many factors besides media communication go into the final decision on whom to vote for.

In the rise and fall of "power models" we also saw the rise and fall of old-style propaganda successes, the bullet theory and opinion leadership theory. (There were others: cognitive dissonance, selective perception, and balance theories.) How could those ideas seem so "right" and, later, so "wrong"? Tan offered this explanation:[2]

> A historical explanation suggests that the effect of mass communication on society can best be understood by analyzing the prevailing social and political climate of the time. The early powerful effects model found its greatest acceptance during war and economic depression, when there were ample opportunities, and the conditions were conducive, for the media to be powerful. . . . During the relative calm and prosperity of the 1950s and early 1960s, media audiences were relatively satisfied with their lives. . . . The powerful effects model became a significant influence on researchers as political and social turmoil enveloped the country in the late 1960s and early 1970s.

Tan said it was also possible that our understanding of the effects of media changed with the advances in techniques of measurement.

One might also suggest that an opinion leadership effect really existed in the 1930s, since in those days the media communicated directly with fewer people. Television was unheard of, radio was in its youth, and literacy was far from universal. People might well have received significant information from influential others. Twenty years later, the number of media had increased dramatically, and the media were much more likely to communicate directly with individuals rather than through opinion leaders.

Similarly, the bullet theory of communication might have been unassailable in the context of its time.

Thus the seeming fluctuation in the wisdom of theory need not be a damning of the field. A fallen theory may have been quite appropriate

---

2. Tan, *Mass Communication*, pp. 5-6.

in one context but not in another. Further, the seeming fallibility of theories no doubt reflects the inadequacy of our social science measures and the complexity of human interaction. We just haven't identified, categorized, and measured the myriad variables that contribute to communication. In a sense, a theorist must be a historian, recognizing periodic contexts (environmental, political, technological) that have bearing on the appropriateness (ability to successfully predict) of a particular line of theory.

To get a better sense of the changing nature of theory, the student should review some early and recent editions of scholarly journals. It probably will become evident that what passed for wisdom 30-50 years ago seems dated now. But the student should bear in mind that a difference between then and now does not mean the earlier "truth" has become "untrue"; rather, it may mean only that truth depends on the context in which one finds it.

EXERCISES

Part A. Using microfilm or bound volumes, refer to early editions (between 1930 and 1950) of *Journalism Quarterly*. Identify any article that deals with the apparent effects of media. In the space provided below, discuss (1) media power implicit in the article (i.e., whether the authors presume the media are very powerful, not very powerful, or moderately powerful) and (2) research methods and measurement techniques. Does the research seem relevant today? If not, why? If the research was repeated today, how would the method differ, or how would the outcome differ?

Part B. Again referring to *Journalism Quarterly*, select a recent article (1970 to present) dealing with media effects or some aspect of theory. In the space provided below, discuss (1) how the article differs from very early *JQ* articles, (2) whether the article deals with ideas that might be context-bound (might not seem so true 20-30 years hence), (3) whether the article uses methods and measures more likely to detect subtleties in data, and (4) any other comparison you would make between "old" and "modern" theory.

Part C. At the discretion of the instructor, this exercise may be repeated with another journal such as *Journal of Broadcasting* or *Public Opinion Quarterly*.

UNIT 14

Message Factors in Persuasion

READING:
C. I. Hovland and W. Mandell. "An Experimental Comparison of Conclusion-Drawing by the Communicator and the Audience." *Journal of Abnormal and Social Psychology* 47(1952):581-88.

The persuasiveness of a communication depends on three broad sets of factors: source factors, message factors, and audience factors. Source factors are addressed in Unit 15. We turn our attention now to message factors.

Research on message factors has concentrated on four main variables: (1) the order of the arguments, (2) whether the presentation is "one-sided" or "two-sided," (3) what kind of appeal is made, and (4) whether a conclusion is implicit or explicit.

1. Order of arguments. If you wish to be persuasive in oral or written communication, how should you structure your argument? Should you lead off with your main premise, and then proceed to back it up with discussion? Or should you build your case carefully, slowly, holding your main statement of position for the end of your presentation? Should you make your main argument early and then repeat it some number of times as you proceed?

2. One-sided vs. two-sided. If you wish to be persuasive, should you tell both sides of the argument, or should you leave the other side to someone else? Would it be better for you simply to state your position and your reasons and not remind the audience there is another point of view?

3. Type of appeal. If you wish to be persuasive, your strategy may be to appeal to a certain need of the listener. For instance, you may decide to use a logical appeal, you may appeal to the pride of the listener, or you may hope to frighten the listener into agreement. What kind of appeal works best? If you appeal to fear, should you use strong fear or just a little fear? (Example: "Smoking will kill you" vs. "Some studies show that people who smoke are more prone to illness.")

4. Conclusion drawing. If you wish to be persuasive, how far do you go in prescribing for the listener what to think about the facts you have presented? Should you spell it out plainly? For example, "Here's what you must do." Or should you (a) merely suggest or imply a conclusion or (b) leave conclusion drawing for the audience (let the facts speak for themselves)?

In this discussion, we did not propose to answer these questions; this will be left to any of several major texts that have reviewed the literature of the field. Here, the purpose is to reinforce the questions and to provide an opportunity for the student to examine actual communications against that background.

EXERCISES

<u>Part A</u>. Clip the lead editorial from a daily newspaper and evaluate it along the lines suggested below. Attach the clipping to this page so your instructor may confirm your assessment if desired.

Order of arguments. Discuss briefly: Where does the main thesis of the editorial appear? Is it repeated? Does the editorial build to a logical point, then spring the "punch line"? Any other comment you would make about the ordering of the presentation?

One-sided vs. two-sided. Discuss briefly: Is the argument all one-sided, or does it attempt to present the whole story?

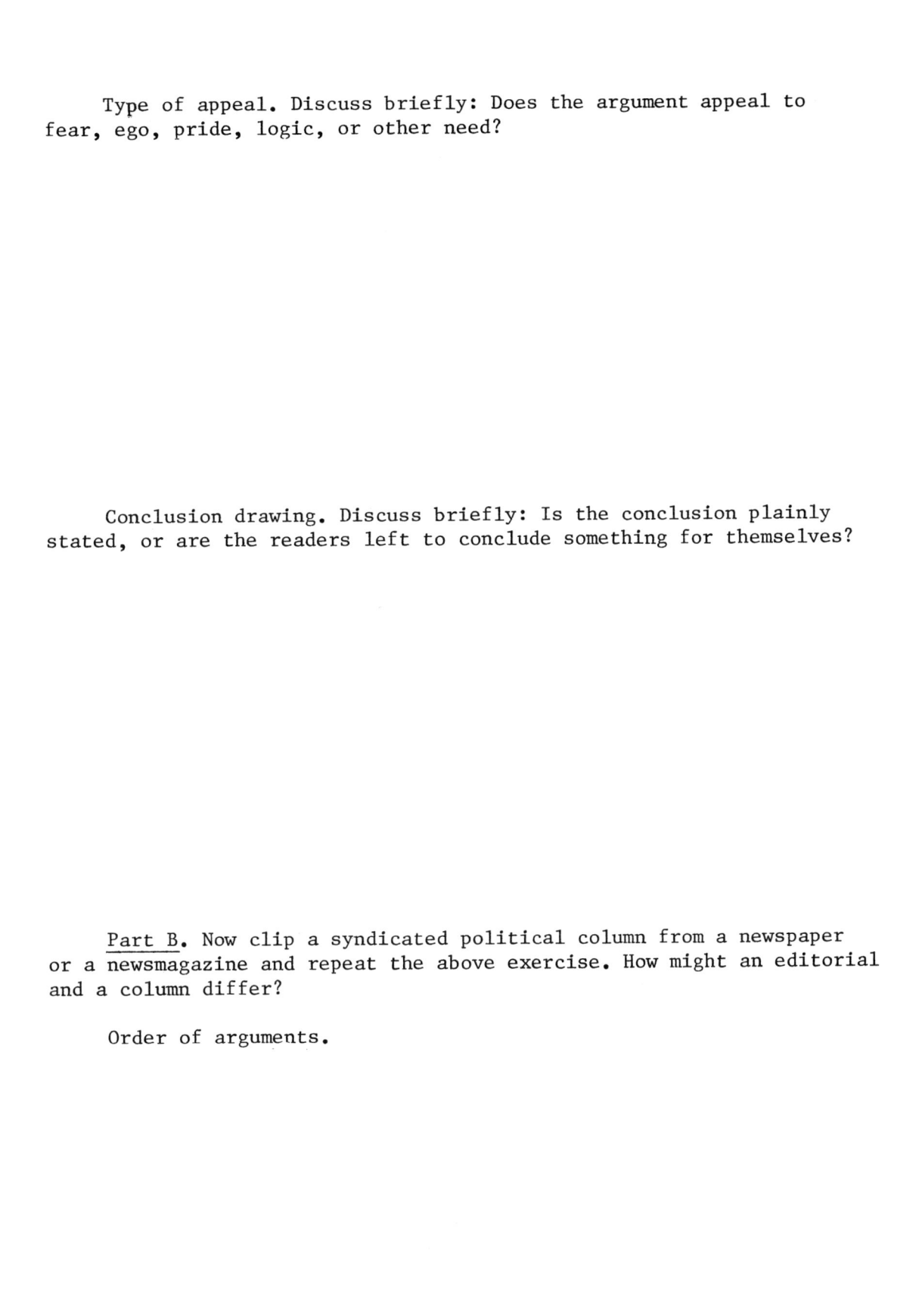

Type of appeal. Discuss briefly: Does the argument appeal to fear, ego, pride, logic, or other need?

Conclusion drawing. Discuss briefly: Is the conclusion plainly stated, or are the readers left to conclude something for themselves?

Part B. Now clip a syndicated political column from a newspaper or a newsmagazine and repeat the above exercise. How might an editorial and a column differ?

Order of arguments.

One-sided vs. two-sided.

Type of appeal.

Conclusion drawing.

UNIT 15 *Source Credibility*

READING:
Carl I. Hovland and Walter Weiss. "The Influence of Source Credibility on Communication Effectiveness." *Public Opinion Quarterly* 15(1951):635-50.

Why was Walter Cronkite, in his latter years as anchor and senior correspondent for CBS-TV News, judged by many as the "most believable man in the world"? If Cronkite read news in competition with another man of similar age, hair color, weight, etc., would the two be of equal believability? Perhaps, but probably not. So we have to ask, What are the qualities we look for in an individual that would lead to trust? Are we conscious of the nature of our judgments? Can our judgments be manipulated by "image builders"?

We are told that Dan Rather, Cronkite's replacement, rated (at least in his early appearances) as a little less believable. It was said he was advised to add a sweater to his customary business suit. The sweater was supposed to give him an aura of warmth and sincerity and less of the "lean and hungry look." The sweater story is an interesting anecdote; it implies both our weakness and our strength. It reflects people's failures and successes in judging others.

That we make judgments is a strength, and the better our judgments, the happier our outcomes. We make judgments by watching others' eyes, how they walk, the words they choose, or the confidence with which they use them. But our judgments can be a weakness too, for they expose our vulnerability to deceit. People are easily led to believe falsehoods. We sometimes perceive sincerity when it is only an act; we perceive wisdom when the speaker may be merely mouthing the words of others.

When we judge others, what qualities do we look for? The following exercises are designed to provide insight into this complex phenomenon. When you have completed the exercises, we will continue the discussion of what the research says about the nature of source credibility.

EXERCISES

Part A. Think of any news reporter who is, for you, the most believable. By "believable" we mean the person you would have the least reason to doubt. The person could represent any medium (television, newspaper, magazine, radio) but should be in news, not entertainment per se. (No attempt will be made at this time to define news; use your own judgment.) When you have identified the person, write the name in the space provided below. Next, write all the adjectives you can think of that describe the qualities you feel make the person you have named believable. (Adjectives include words such as "handsome or pretty, smart, pedagogical," etc.) There may be a large number; certainly there should be 8 to 10 or more. If we have not provided sufficient spaces, add your own.

Name of reporter _____

Medium represented _____

Adjectives

_____ _____ _____ _____
_____ _____ _____ _____
_____ _____ _____ _____
_____ _____ _____ _____
_____ _____ _____ _____

Part B. Now that you have completed your list of adjectives, let's group the words that seem to be related. Look again at your list; some of the words, even though different from each other, are likely (but not necessarily) to be similar to some others; that is, some are based on roughly the same kinds of feelings or meanings. For example, if you described your news source (the reporter) as both well-spoken and articulate, you would probably agree that the two terms are somewhat related. Group all the related terms. If you identified, say, 15 different adjectives, you might put them into any number of groups from 1 to 15. Each group may be home for 1 to 6 words. In the spaces that follow, try your hand at grouping your adjectives. (Example: Group 1--articulate, well-spoken, resonant, understandable. You can see that each of these terms relates to a person's ability to communicate effectively.)

Group 1   Group 2   Group 3   Group 4

| Group 5 | Group 6 | Group 7 | Group 8 |

| Group 9 | Group 10 | Group 11 | Group 12 |

Part C. When you have placed each of your adjectives in one group or another, but not in more than one, go back and count the number of adjectives in each. Let us assume for a moment that there is significance in the number of adjectives per group; few adjectives means a not very well-developed cognition, although not necessarily an unimportant one. (For instance, if your group 4 has only two or three words, but group 2 has five, we will assume group 2 is a more fully developed cognition.) Rank the groups according to the number of adjectives in each. The group with the most is "1", and the group with the second most adjectives is "2", etc. Let us further assume that these rankings are related to the strength of feelings you may have for the qualities identified by the group of terms. In other words, we want to assume that the ranks of your groups represent your most important factors in credibility. Are we making a satisfactory assumption? Why?

Now that you have formed groups of words, you should examine the words in your group 1 and devise a single term that captures the essential meanings implied by the collection of words. Look back at the example provided; you will see four terms, all related to articulation and each dealing with some aspect of communication. But "communication" may be too vague, too general, to adequately describe the four terms; perhaps "articulation" would better capture the combination of meanings. Can you identify a better term? Continue your examination of your groups of adjectives until you have identified a single concept to represent each.

As you can see, this kind of analysis becomes subjective, and its success depends on the ingenuity and judgment (and of course the ethics) of the researcher. But further, the exercise has involved a sample of one person, and we will see in another exercise (see Unit 31) that the margin of error for a sample of one can be very great indeed. This exercise on credibility can be expanded by grouping the responses of the full class. But, if your own groups and concepts represent the feelings of a large group, what will they show? They will show that the credibility of a news reporter depends (at least in some measure) on the characteristics identified. In other words, if you want to enhance the credibility of your reporter, you will examine the headings of your groups of terms and measure the extent to which your reporter embodies those characteristics. You may even ask the reporter to change, to meet the standards you wish to emphasize.

In rough form, the exercise you have completed illustrates the manner in which much credibility research data have been gathered and the way in which the data have been put to use in the marketplace.

NATURE OF SOURCE CREDIBILITY

Back to Walter Cronkite and Dan Rather. If we knew the qualities that their audience perceived for highly credible reporters, could we employ those qualities in either changing our staff or in hiring new staff? For instance, if we found that reporters' "warmth" (probably defined as sincerity or feeling for others) was important, could we improve the reporters' credibility by having him or her wear a sweater? Many researchers think so, and that is the approach much research has taken.

Much of the research on source credibility has used a statistical technique called "factor analysis." This is an important statistical concept and is referred to in several of the exercises. Factor analysis involves the correlation and intercorrelation of variables, but essentially it is a reduction technique. It reduces a large data set to a smaller set of derived factors. We use it to identify underlying mathematical relationships between variables. In so doing, we identify groups of variables that are related. For example, if you identified 20 or 100 adjectives relating to source credibility, you could reduce the subjectivity of the evaluation by using factor analysis. The factor analysis computer program could do for you what you did for yourself and do it with mathematical precision.

Using factor analysis, Andersen identified an "evaluative" factor in source credibility, characterized by honest, moral, fair, sympathetic, reasonable, and likable and a "dynamism" factor characterized by interesting, strong, fast, aggressive, and active.[1] Presented with the same clusters of variables, would you have named them "evaluation" and "dynamism"? Berlo and Lemert also identified a "dynamism" factor but also two other important ones: competence and trustworthiness.[2] Lemert,

---

1. Kenneth Andersen, "An Experimental Study of the Interaction of Artistic and Non-Artistic Ethos in Persuasion," unpublished Ph.D. dissertation, University of Wisconsin, Madison, 1961.
2. David K. Berlo and James B. Lemert, "A Factor Analytic Study of the Dimensions of Source Credibility," paper presented to the 1961 convention of the Speech Association of America, New York.

in yet an earlier study, identified other factors, including "safety" (characterized by honest, open-minded, safe, objective) and "qualification" (characterized by trained, experienced, informed, educated).[3] McCroskey identified "authoritativeness" (characterized by reliable, informed, qualified, intelligent, valuable, expert) and "character" (characterized by honest, friendly, pleasant, unselfish, nice, virtuous).[4]

From this brief review, you can see that different researchers used the same technique, factor analysis, to obtain somewhat different outcomes. For instance, the word "honest" appeared in three different factors (evaluation, safety, and character). To a large extent, the different outcomes may be attributed to different input. For example, if there are no "hostile" scales in a data set, there will be no "hostility" factor in the output. Most of the early factor research involved a relatively small number of variables, partly because the popular computer programs handled only a small number of variables. Not intended as an end to all such restriction, research by Singletary nevertheless attempted to get around the problem of limited variables.[5]

In that research, a class of 90 students wrote all the words they could think of that described a credible news source. Another class of 181 students used those terms in opposite-adjective form (good-bad) to rate their most credible news source. The data were run on a program that allowed for 198 variables, a number that would produce thousands of intercorrelations. Factor analysis reduced the set to six major factors accounting for 48% of the variance and another 10 factors that increased the variance to 61%. The primary factors were knowledgeability, attraction, trustworthiness, articulation, hostility, and stability. Minor factors included frankness, sensitivity, effectiveness, dynamism, professional demeanor, perceptiveness, awareness, and confidence. Credibility was found not to be a simple, well-defined system of factors but a highly complex and rather undifferentiated system of factors.

Of course, credibility also depends on whom you ask. The subjects in most social research are students. Variables that contribute to student perceptions of credibility may or may not be the same as those of the nonstudent population of a given community. Media supervisors often call research firms to run elaborate surveys of their own to learn what the local folk think about their communicators. They use the data to make hiring decisions and to structure news and entertainment programs.

---

3. James B. Lemert, cited in Harry C. Triandis, *Attitudes and Attitude Change* (New York: Wiley, 1971).

4. James C. McCroskey and R. E. Dunham, "Ethos: A Compounding Element in Communication Research," *Speech Monographs* 33(1966):456-63.

5. Michael W. Singletary, "Components of Credibility of a Favorable News Source," *Journalism Quarterly* 53(1976):316-19.

UNIT 16
Group Dynamics

READING:
Alex Bavelas. "Communication Patterns in Task-Oriented Groups." In Harold D. Lasswell and Daniel Lerner, eds., *The Policy Sciences*. Stanford, Calif.: Stanford University Press, 1951.

H. J. Leavitt. "Effects of Certain Communication Patterns on Group Performance." *Journal of Abnormal and Social Psychology* 46(1951):38-50.

Robert B. Zajonc. "Effect of Feedback and Probability of Group Success on Individual and Group Performance." *Human Relations* 15(1962):149-61.

It is said that groups have a dynamic of their own, leading to behavioral outcomes distinct from those of individuals. For instance, you can probably imagine a mob scene or a riot in which a crowd is incited to frenzy; individuals caught up in the spirit of the moment participate in activities they normally would avoid. Or perhaps you can recall a theater comedy in which the crowd was caught up in uproarious laughter, while the same comedy might have been not nearly so funny when seen on the home television screen. Some variation of the principle of group behavior applies when groups are called on to reach a consensus involving risk. The mean of the individual decisions might be different from the score obtained when the same individuals are asked to produce a single score for the group. Often the group decision is either more cautious or more risky than that of the individual acting alone. (The direction of the difference depends on the makeup of the group.) The point is simply that the group may be different from the individual; the group has a dynamic.

EXERCISE

After you have done the assigned reading, your instructor may ask you to participate in a discussion exercise illustrating group dynamics.[1]

---

1. Note to instructor: See Teacher's Manual, Group Dynamics, for exercise on this topic.

UNIT 17

Diffusion of Information

READING:
Richard Budd, Malcolm MacLean, Jr., and Arthur M. Barnes. "Regularities in the Diffusion of 2 Major News Events." *Journalism Quarterly* 43(1966):221-30.

Rebecca Quarles, Leo W. Jeffres, Carlos Sanchez-Flundain, and Kurt Nenwirth. "News Diffusion of Assassination Attempts on President Reagan and Pope John Paul II. *Journal of Broadcasting* 27(1983):387-94.

For most of the history of media, the presumption was made that the media communicated directly with people and that persuasive communications moved them to act. That was why monarchs in the early history of printing resorted to licensure and censorship, and that was why they developed the principle of seditious libel, wherein the greater the truth, the greater the libel. Although seditious libel was removed from colonial law shortly after the Revolution, belief in press power remained over the years. Politicians well into the 1800s created and supported their own presses, much as western movie characters hired the fast gun, to blow away the opposition with persuasive words. And then in the early 1900s, it was evident to nearly everyone that the presses of the world were important in marshaling strength to finish the task of the "war to end all wars" (World War I).

But in the 1940s, Lazarsfeld, Berelson, and Gaudet began to observe that the media did not always speak directly to people; sometimes the media spoke to opinion leaders who transmitted the message to others. If this was the case, the media might not be as powerful as previously believed. The media message might be "laundered" through the selection processes of the opinion leaders. So instead of message A leading to behavior B, message A might be filtered and refracted, as with light through a prism, the line of the light depending on the position of the prism. Filtering of messages was a revelation that created a stir in research circles continuing for 20 years. But instead of being confirmed, the idea of opinion leadership (the two-step flow of information) simply became more complex. The two steps became multisteps, and then it seemed everyone was an opinion leader. If everyone was an opinion leader, what benefit would the theory provide? Opinion leadership research heard its death knell in 1968, the end of an era, an interesting idea "down the tube."

But out of opinion leadership research grew another research tradition, diffusion. Diffusion refers to spread, and diffusion can involve both innovations and information. We will concentrate on information diffusion in this unit. Clearly, the idea is a first cousin to opinion leadership, for we are asking, Where do people get their news? Whom do they talk to about it? There is another question: Why are people interested in news and in spreading it and what is gratifying about news? But that is another problem. Keep reading.

Are we all about equally likely to diffuse information such as a shooting, an election outcome, a fire downtown? No? Well, what are the characteristics of diffusers? Do they read/watch/listen more to news than the rest of us? Are they smarter, do they have a particular language background, etc.? We ask these questions because if we knew or could reasonably predict the most likely diffusers and knew which of them were most likely to be influential, we might be able to achieve important communications outside conventional media channels. If you can identify diffusers and can tap into their transmissions, you can communicate to others who are more difficult to reach.

EXERCISES

Part A. To learn whether we are equals in the arena of diffusion, let's do a little polling. If we assume the reader is part of a classroom of students and if each student interviews a number of carefully selected people outside the class, the cumulation might reveal interesting patterns. In this exercise, we will offer a brief questionnaire; it will require only a very few minutes to answer. (It may be duplicated or revised to meet the needs of the class.)

At the outset, it will be necessary for you and the instructor to identify a news topic to study. That in itself raises questions: Is diffusion different for local/national/international stories on the basis of such aspects as proximity and salience? What characteristics of a story make it likely to stimulate diffusion? Your instructor will help you decide whether to try to answer such questions or to put them off until another day. In any event, identify a news event and decide which person(s) you will interview. You might draw your sample from the student directory; if there is not one, you might select each nth person in a dorm. Or perhaps you would prefer to work with a nonstudent sample. Simply decide in the classroom how many responses are required and how they are to be obtained.

When data are in, compile them to see whether diffusion is a function of variables such as sex, origin of information, frequency of news use, etc.

Tabulation of diffusion data. Each interviewer might interview 5-10 people or more at the discretion of the instructor. In a class of 15 people, this would generate 75-150+ responses. Although tabulation may seem unwieldy, it may be accomplished readily. Each student should tabulate his or her own data and provide that to the instructor on request. The instructor, aided by a student with a pocket calculator, can then compile the data on the blackboard. The purpose of the tabulation will be (1) to learn where the respondents got their news first and (2) to obtain a description of the diffusers. Responses can be broken out on several demographic variables. Blackboard tables and tallies such as the following are suggested.

SOURCE OF NEWS

	Media Male (freq./ %)	Media Female (freq./ %)		Interpersonal Male (freq./ %)	Interpersonal Female (freq./ %)
TV			Stranger		
Radio			Family		
Newspaper			Friend		
Magazine			Colleague		
Other			Other		
Total			Total		

QUESTIONNAIRE

Diffusion of Information: How News Gets Around

Interviewer reads the following to respondent:

There was a story (on TV, on radio, in newspaper, etc.) today that said (quote whatever story you choose). We are conducting a survey (on campus, in this town, etc.) to find whether people already know of this story and, if they do, how they learned of it. We would appreciate your allowing us to ask just a few simple questions.

1. Recall the news event we described to you. Had you heard of it before we spoke to you? ___no ___yes (if no, skip to question 7)

2. Can you recall where you first learned of this news?
___media ___interpersonal Explain:_____

3. If you first heard the news from someone other than a news reporter, was that someone

      ___a stranger
      ___a member of the family
      ___a friend
      ___a colleague at work
      ___other (please explain)_____

4. If you received the news first through conventional media channels, did you get the news first from

      ___newspaper
      ___radio
      ___TV
      ___other

5. Since you heard the news, have you spoken with anyone else about that particular news? ___yes ___no (if no, skip to question 7)

6. If you have spoken with someone else about the news, did the other person already know, or were you the first to tell the person?

      ___already knew
      ___was first to tell the person

To help us sort out the answers, we need to know just a little bit about you:

7. _____(If a student, your major) (if a nonstudent, your occupation)

8. _____How often do you read a newspaper?

9. _____How often do you watch TV news (local or national)?

10. _____How often do you listen to radio news?

11. _____Did you vote in the last presidential or congressional election?

Thank you very much.

Part B. Part A involved asking other people their experience with transmitting or receiving news. What about your own experience in the past two to three days? Have you offered or received news? Conduct the following brief self-inventory:

1. Has someone in the past two to three days commented to you about a news event?

      ___yes ___no ___can't recall (don't give up too easily!)

2. What was the news? _____

3. Can you group the news item in some broad category(ies) such as (a) military, (b) education, (c) social problem, (d) public affairs/politics, (e) accidents/disasters, etc.? Circle the correct category or write the category here:

_____

4. Since you heard the news, have you spoken to anyone else about it?

___yes ___no   explain: _____

_____

Part C. Finally, as a critique of this type of research, identify what you see as some problems. How accurate are the data you collected? What kinds of questions should be asked? Are interviews effective two to three days after a news event? Is survey research the best method of studying diffusion of news? Do not necessarily limit your critique to consideration of these questions; add your own. Use the space below.

UNIT 18
Diffusion of Innovation

READING:
Bernard Berelson and Ronald Freedman. "A Study in Fertility Control." *Scientific American* 210(1964):29-37.

Alfredo D. Mendez. "Social Structure and the Diffusion of Innovation." *Human Organization* 27(1968):241-49.

Herbert Menzel and Elihu Katz. "Social Relations and Innovation in the Medical Profession: The Epidemiology of a New Drug." *Public Opinion Quarterly* 19(1955-56):337-52.

Everette M. Rogers and F. Floyd Shoemaker. *Communication of Innovations: A Cross-Cultural Approach*. New York: The Free Press, 1971.

Another approach to investigating the flow of news from its source to its audience destination is studying the diffusion of innovation. Instead of considering news and information as the commodity being exchanged, researchers have considered how a new product or a new way of doing a certain task is adopted in a society.

There are a few good reasons why communication theorists find studying diffusion of "innovations" beneficial in understanding the diffusion of "information." First, there is a similarity between a breaking news story and the introduction of a new product; as far as the public is concerned, both come seemingly from nowhere. Second, the mass media play a prominent role in making the public aware of the existence of the information or the product. Third, the mass media (whether through news stories and features or through advertising) help explain the information or the product. Finally, the pattern of public recognition and of possible acceptance of the information or new product can be highly similar. So theorists have borrowed from diffusion of innovation research to establish conditions for acceptance of a new product or idea and have argued that similar conditions might apply to the recognition and acceptance of news and information.

Rogers's research has provided the following considerations about diffusion of innovation:

1. There are four stages to adoption of innovations: (a) knowledge, (b) persuasion, (c) decision, and (d) confirmation.

2. People who know about the innovation early are of higher socioeconomic status: (a) who have more mass media and interpersonal communication exposure, (b) who have more "change agent" contact, and (c) who are more cosmopolitan.

3. Most individuals know about some innovation they don't consider adopting because they don't see it as relevant to their needs.

4. Consideration by an individual of adopting any innovation depends first on general attitude toward change and then on attitude toward the specific innovation.

5. Upon learning of an innovation and then considering adoption, individuals engage in a "vicarious trial" by projecting how the innovation might affect them.

6. Most individuals won't adopt an innovation without trying it for a probationary period first. Those innovations that don't offer a small-scale trial will be adopted more slowly.

7. Each step in the adoption process is a potential rejection point.

8. Six attributes of innovations are (a) relative advantage, or how much better is it than what it will be replacing; (b) affordability; (c) its compatibility with existing values; (d) its complexity, or how difficult is it to understand and use; (e) ease of trial; and (f) ease of observation, or degree to which the innovation can be explained to others.

9. Mass media can't be relied upon to communicate about complex innovations.

10. There is a "diffusion effect," which means that the more widely accepted the innovation is, the more pressure there is on others to accept it as well.

11. There are distinct adopter categories. Innovators, some 2.5% of the population, are anxious to try new ideas; they are venturesome and likely to maintain contact with other innovators. Early adopters (13.5%) are local opinion leaders who are respected by others and maintain that respect by discreet use of innovations. The early majority (34%) are characterized as "deliberate." They have high interpersonal communication among peers but are not leaders. The late majority (34%) are skeptical and cautious. They don't adopt until most others have done so. Laggards (16%) are traditional, socially isolated, locally oriented, and without opinion leadership.

Using the above information about the diffusion of innovation, complete the following exercise about the adoption of videocassette recording devices (VCRs); (Note: the instructor may wish to substitute some other items or innovations here.)

EXERCISE

1. Do you or your family possess a VCR? ___yes ___no

2. If so, how long have you had it? _____

   Whether or not you have one, complete the remainder:

3. Can a VCR
   a. record an over-the-air TV program? ___yes ___no
   b. record a TV program on cable? ___yes ___no
   c. record when no one is at home? ___yes ___no
   d. record two programs simultaneously? ___yes ___no
   e. record one station while the viewer is watching another station? ___yes ___no
   f. record over an already recorded tape? ___yes ___no

4. Approximately how much does a VCR cost? _____

5. Approximately how much does a blank VCR tape cost? _____

Considering your knowledge of VCRs as a mass media technological innovation, complete the following based on diffusion of innovation theory:

6. VCRs have high relative advantage.   agree /__/__/__/__/__/ disagree

7. VCRs are generally affordable.   agree /__/__/__/__/__/ disagree

8. VCRs are compatible with TV users' values.   agree /__/__/__/__/__/ disagree

9. VCRs are highly complex.   agree /__/__/__/__/__/ disagree

10. VCRs offer small-trial experimentation.   agree /__/__/__/__/__/ disagree

11. VCRs offer high observability.   agree /__/__/__/__/__/ disagree

12. At what stage of investigation might we expect the potential adopter to actually purchase a VCR?

13. Under what circumstances might we expect the potential adopter to reject the VCR innovation?

14. Describe the kind of individual who might have been among the first to purchase a VCR within a year after they became available on the market (about 1978).

15. Describe the kind of individual who might be among the last to purchase a VCR or who might never purchase one.

UNIT 19
Agenda Setting

READING:
Maxwell McCombs and Donald Shaw. "The Agenda-Setting Function of the Mass Media." *Public Opinion Quarterly* 36(1972):176-87.

During the 1970s the single most researched notion in mass communications theory involved what is called "agenda setting." The term was coined by McCombs and Shaw. Their article was based on interviews and media analysis from the 1968 presidential election. They noted a strong relationship between media content and people's identification of what they saw as "the issues" in the campaign. In other words, the media seemed to set the agenda (the standards for what was important) for public discussion.

Notice this distinction: McCombs and Shaw posited *not* that the media suggested what people should think about the issues but only the issues they would think about. This was a new approach, since most previous research began with the presumption that the media were doing something to people, a behavioral approach. And although the 1968 research project had shortcomings (the sample was very small and the conclusion did not make clear whether media set public agendas or the public set media agendas), the idea was intuitively appealing. Since publication of the original work, other researchers have contributed dozens of variations and extensions. Agenda setting seems to be withstanding the test of both time and research and seems to be slipping quietly into the realm of accepted wisdom, notwithstanding important questions that remain unresolved.

For the student, it may be useful now to reconstruct the original McCombs-Shaw project, or rather something akin to it. The intent of the exercise is to demonstrate the statistical method and the concept behind the research design. The research method is relatively simple. It is based on "correlation," a statistical technique that allows the researcher to derive mathematically the relationships between variables. For example, correlation would be expected between height and weight; weight should increase with height. Correlation, ranging from zero to plus or minus one, would give a measure of the extent to which height and weight vary together. If weight had no relationship to height, the correlation might be zero; if weight increased moderately with height, the correlation might be in the .35 to .60 range; if weight increased directly with height, the correlation would exceed, say, .75 but would not exceed 1.0.

But before McCombs and Shaw could compute their correlations, they were required to obtain data:

1. They interviewed a sample of independent voters in Chapel Hill, N.C., and they asked the voters to identify what they saw as the most important issues of the 1968 political campaign. Then the voters were asked to rank the issues, that is, to put the number 1 by the most important issue, the number 2 by the second most important, etc.
2. They studied the content of media available to the people of Chapel Hill; they categorized and counted the stories in newspapers and on TV and radio.
3. They defined news items as either "major" or "minor." For newspapers, a major news item was one that appeared in the lead position on page one or one that carried a three-column or greater headline. The plan was to study the correlation between voters' rankings of issues and the media's (apparent) ranking of the same issues.

EXERCISES

So the student will be in a better position to evaluate the results of such research, let's construct a research situation. We won't insist on the rigor McCombs and Shaw required, so we should interpret our results with great reserve. Still, the exercise should provide insights into the wisdom of the idea, and it should provide at least a rough picture of the method of the original research.

First, we will suggest two data-gathering techniques (survey and content analysis); then we will discuss statistical analysis of the data.

Part A. The following questionnaire may be filled out by students in a class, or the instructor may wish to have members of the class interview selected others. Note that the exercise may be conducted with as much or as little scientific rigor as the instructor deems feasible.

QUESTIONNAIRE

To the Respondent:
1. Suppose a senatorial or presidential election was now in progress. What major national issues today would be likely to dominate the political debate? By issues, we mean items of concern or controversy. Your answers should represent what you feel are the issues, not what you think someone else feels. In the spaces below, list at least five such issues but as many others as you wish.

_____   _____

_____   _____

_____   _____

_____   _____

_____   _____

    2. Suppose there was a local election for city council in progress now; what local issues would be likely to dominate the debate? In the spaces below, identify as many local issues as you can that would relate to an election if the local election was held today.

_____   _____

_____   _____

_____   _____

_____   _____

_____   _____

    3. Demographics: (modify as necessary to fit needs of sample)

        a. your class standing: ___frosh___soph___junior___senior
        b. registered to vote? ___yes___no
        c. political affiliation? ___repub___demo___indep___other
        d. interest in politics? ___extremely___mildly___very little ___couldn't care less
        e. In your own estimate, where do you get most of your news? ___newspapers___magazines___TV___radio___other

(Optional: If a presidential election is approaching, ask the respondent to identify major contenders and to rank them. This can be used in connection with Part B.)

    Part B. Survey Tally and Content Analysis. The survey has three purposes: (1) to identify public "issues," (2) to rank-order public issues on the basis of importance, and (3) to correlate these with media content.

    Achieving point 1 is easy. Students should simply tell the instructor the issues named by the respondents, and the instructor will write them on the blackboard. Some related issues may be combined (to keep the list short). The final list of issues probably should not exceed 10 to 15.

Point 2 is also easy. The instructor will point to each issue on the board and ask for a show of hands as to how many respondents named that issue. We will assume that the issue mentioned most often is the one that is most important. Rank-order all issues in that manner. (Note: The questionnaire could be altered to ask respondents to rank their issues; in that case, the average rank per issue would establish the ranks.)

Point 3 is a little tougher, but manageable. We want to learn whether the public agenda is the same as the media agenda. We already know (from the survey) the public agenda, so now we need the media agenda. We will concentrate on print media; it would be possible to include broadcasting, but we want to keep this simple. Armed with coding forms representing each of the public issues, each student would examine a carefully selected set of newspapers. The students would document (on the form) the occurrence of each type of story. When the study is finished and all stories are coded, the figures can be tallied.

If the public and media agendas are the same, then the issue mentioned most frequently in the survey will be the one seen most often in the newspaper.

Table 19.1 shows how the data would be displayed for correlation. Table 19.2 provides a coding form for agenda-setting content analysis.

Table 19.1. Displaying Data for Correlation

Issues Identified in Survey, Ranked by Frequency of Mention	Issues Identified in Newspapers, Ranked by Frequency of Occurrence
1. Inflation[a]	1. Energy
2. Communism	2. Inflation
3. Energy	3. Communism
4. Crime	4. Crime
5. Government spending	5. Government spending

[a]The correspondence is imperfect; nevertheless, the correlation may be high because the ranks are not widely different.

Table 19.2. Coding Form for Agenda-setting Content Analysis

Campaign Issue Being Coded (e.g., environment)	Headline	Newspaper Name	Publication Date	Page Number	Number of Paragraphs	Number of Columns
1.						
2.						
3.						
4.						
5.						
6.						
7.						
8.						
9.						
10.						
11.						
12.						

Part C. Statistical Procedure. Here is the formula for Spearman's rank order correlation if the student or instructor wishes to complete the statistical analysis.

$$Rho = 1 - \frac{6 \Sigma D^2}{n(n^2 - 1)}$$

where D = difference score between each pair of scores
n = number of pairs of scores
Σ = the sum of squares

Details of statistical procedure:

1. In one column, list the issues identified in the survey and rank them by frequency of mention; see Table 19.1.
2. In the next column, list the issues identified in newspapers and rank them by frequency of occurrence.

3. Subtract the frequency rank (column 2) from the issue rank (column 1) for each pair.

4. Square all the differences and add the squares. Call this the sum of squares.

5. Now, as in the formula, multiply the sum of squares by 6; we will get back to this below.

6. Calculate $n(n^2 - 1)$; recall, n = number of pairs of scores. So if we have 7 issues and 7 frequencies, n = 7. Example: 7 × 7 - 1 = 48; 7 × 48 = 336.

7. Again with the formula, divide 6 times the sum of squares by $n(n^2 - 1)$.

8. The number you obtain by dividing will be less than one. As a final step in the formula, subtract that number from the number 1; presto, there is your correlation.

9. Enter rho (correlation) here:_____

10. Is it low, moderate, or high?_____

When you have obtained the data and completed the statistical analysis, what do you have? What does your correlation "mean"? Well, it means that, to the extent of the observed correlation, the two sets of ranks varied together. That is, the issues that citizens identified as issues tended to be the same as issues emphasized by the media. The essential point is that the media tend to tell us what is important and what to talk about. In other words, media set our agenda for public issues. Or do they?

The counterargument, of course, is that the media don't set the agenda, the people do; and the media are merely playing the tune that the public calls for. It seems to be a question of which came first, the chicken or the egg. But maybe that is not the important question. Maybe the importance of the idea is that if certain issues show up as the most important, the most emphasized, they needn't have. In other words, maybe we miss genuinely important issues and instead have our agendas focused on issues that sell news. That has been a criticism of political campaigns for decades. Surely there are many important public policy issues that receive precious little media emphasis. Hence, we have to ask, if the media set the agenda (or even if the public sets the agenda and the media merely follow), is it the "right" agenda? Is it the one that will maximize public well-being? This is the question that grows from research on agenda setting.

UNIT 20
The Cultivation Hypothesis

READING:
Anthony Doob and Glenn E. Macdonald. "Television Viewing and Fear of Victimization: Is the Relationship Causal?" *Journal of Personality and Social Psychology* 37(1979):170-79.

George Gerbner and Larry Gross. "Living with Television: The Violence Profile." *Journal of Communication* 26(1976):173-99.

Michael Morgan. "Heavy Television Viewing and Perceived Quality of Life." *Journalism Quarterly* 61(1984):499-504, 740.

A relatively recent theme in mass communication theory deals with a very broad view of mass media effects on individuals and society. The theory has been discussed variously in terms of "cultural norms," "popular culture," and recently the "cultivation hypothesis." The basic tenet of the theory is that mass media influence is subtle but pervasive. Over time, depending on what themes are prevalent in media content, people's attitudes change somewhat toward the message implicit in the themes. Importantly, the presumption follows that heavy media users experience more of the change than light users.

The hypothesis is not that mass media purposely attempt to alter people's perceptions. But the hypothesis does predict that a heavy media user's "world view" will be altered toward acceptance of the dominant themes carried by the media. As an analogy, let's look at the recent history of popular music. Research has shown that pop music lyrics have moved steadily (since the early 1950s) from hand-holding notions of love and romance to direct expression of physical attraction, from distant dreams to one-night stands. Lyrics have urged self-discovery and self-expression (sometimes through drugs) and deemphasized social conventions. Cultivation theory would predict that frequent listeners to the music are likely to have been the most attuned to (in agreement with) the themes portrayed.

That is not to say that heavy users are necessarily more likely to behave in ways suggested by music lyrics; no doubt you are personally acquainted with many who are heavy users and are extremely "straight." But there are two other ways to look at the matter. One has to do with probabilities. Let's say that X number of deviant behaviors would occur regardless of the existence of the stimulus at hand. The question for the researcher, then, is this: Is the number of occurrences larger than would happen by chance alone? And finally, can the difference be attributed to the supposed stimulus, or are there plausible rival possibilities? In plain terms, if young people are using drugs, is it attributable to stimuli such as music lyrics, or is the behavior better explained by some other social factors?

The other way to look at the effect of media cultivation is as an agent of gradual change. Let's all agree that we don't behave in a new manner just because it is proposed; yet, if the proposition is widespread (as media make it), it may take on a legitimizing quality. One might come to think, "This must be OK because I'm hearing it so much, and other people are hearing the same things." Only in the past decade or so have studies been done that document the cultural norms or "cultivation" perspective. George Gerbner of the Annenberg School of Communications at the University of Pennsylvania has published a number of articles dealing with violence on television and its effect on the world view of heavy users.[1] This research argues (not all researchers agree) that those who are heavy TV viewers, those who watch more than four hours a day, consider the world more sinister than do light users. With the high percentage of TV drama focused on police and law enforcement activities, the heavy viewers have accepted many of the themes they have seen. Heavy viewers are likely to overestimate the percentage of the population who work in law enforcement and their own chances of being involved in some violent activity during the coming week and are generally less trusting of other people.

The idea of "cultural norms" or "cultivation" is a powerful media theory, that is, it attributes great power to the mass media, although in this case the effect is in attitudes and is cumulative over time. If media have this effect on people, we may predict the mass media will be responsible for subtle shifts in attitude over time. In other words, "What you see is what you get." We might even predict that the direction of attitude change is likely to be toward personal gratification and personal freedom, provided some counterforce does not alter the themes we presently see emphasized in media. In any event, we can count on media to deal with changing social themes.

For example, the media in recent years have carried articles on America's homosexual population. Coverage began in news reports but since has included situation comedy and drama. Previously depiction of homosexual lifestyles (when they were depicted at all) had been derisive. In cultivation theory, we would predict that heavy media users would be most likely to hold favorable attitudes toward homosexuality, or at least to hold attitudes that are more tolerant than those held by the general population.

---

1. George Gerbner, M. Jackson-Beeck, S. Jeffries, and N. Signorielli, "Cultural Indicators: Violence Profile No. 9," *Journal of Communication* 28(1978):176-207.

EXERCISES

Part A. Consider the cultivation hypothesis as expressed above and write a paragraph below on attitudes the American public might have about marriage based on the public's heavy media use during the past 10 to 20 years. Can you provide facts (strong evidence such as survey data) rather than merely speculating about changing attitudes toward marriage as an institution in this social system? Does the cultivation hypothesis hold?

Part B. Consider the social institutions or aspects of modern society listed below and complete the check sheet that follows it.

92

ASPECTS OF MODERN SOCIETY

Working women
Medical care
Computers (new technology)
Political parties
Labor unions
Elementary schools
High schools
Atomic energy as fuel source
Professional sports
Nursing homes
The environment
Prisons
Unidentified flying objects

Child abuse
Divorce
Taxes
Alcohol abuse
Congress
Religion
The family
Urban living
The military
The atomic bomb
The mass media
Illegal aliens
Safe driving

CULTIVATION HYPOTHESIS CHECK SHEET

From the list of aspects of modern society above, select the six you believe would provide the greatest measure of attitude differences if you were making a random national sample of the American population, then contrast the opinions of heavy vs. light media users.

When you have selected the six topics you think would show the most differentiation among media-user types, record the rating you think each type would give on the following scale:

very positive /___/___/___/___/___/ very negative
                 5   4   3   2   1

In the appropriate column, mark the number of the rating (as illustrated on the example) you think each media-user type would give to the topics you list in the blanks below.

Topic	Heavy Media Users	Light Media Users
1. _____	_____	_____
2. _____	_____	_____
3. _____	_____	_____
4. _____	_____	_____
5. _____	_____	_____
6. _____	_____	_____

Below, give some reasons why you chose the first two topics:

Topic 1:_____

_____

_____

Topic 2:_____

_____

_____

Part C. Please answer the following questions. Do not discuss your responses with your classmates; your responses should be your own.

1. Please give your best estimate of how much time per day you spend watching television (your estimate to the nearest half-hour):_____

2. When you watch TV, do you have a preference for a particular kind of program? Indicate from the following list:

    a. sit-com   d. talk show   g. game show   j. no preference
    b. cinema   e. sports   h. other
    c. action-drama f. soaps   i. news/weather

(If you indicated "other," please be specific:_____)

3. Do you watch TV mostly (if you watch at all) in the

    a. mornings (6 A.M. to noon)
    b. afternoons (noon to 6 P.M.)
    c. evenings (6 P.M. to 11:30)
    d. late nights (11:30 to 6 A.M.)

4. Please indicate your sex: male____   female____

Now we want to ask you a few questions about your perceptions of the possibility of violence in your daily life.

1. To what extent do you agree with the statement that "Most people can be trusted"? (Response options follow.)

____ strongly agree

____ agree

____ undecided

____ disagree

____ strongly disagree

2. In any given week, what are your chances of being involved in some type of violence?

    a. about 1 in 10   d. about 1 in 75
    b. about 1 in 25   e. about 1 in 100 or more
    c. about 1 in 50

3. What do you think the chances are that if you were to walk alone in the vicinity of where you live that you would be the victim of a crime?

    a. about 1 in 10   d. about 1 in 75
    b. about 1 in 25   e. about 1 in 100 or more
    c. about 1 in 50

4. How safe are children in your town or city?

    a. ____ extremely safe   d. ____ not very safe

    b. ____ very safe   e. ____ extremely unsafe

    c. ____ somewhat safe

5. How comfortable would you be in walking alone downtown at night?

    a. ____ extremely comfortable   d. ____ not very comfortable

    b. ____ very comfortable   e. ____ extremely uncomfortable

    c. ____ somewhat comfortable

If you have been candid and thoughtful in your responses to these questions, you may be interested to learn how your perceptions compare with those of your classmates. You may also be interested to learn whether, as Gerbner suggested, heavy media use is associated with perceptions of greater danger. Your instructor will lead a tally of the results.

UNIT 21
Media Uses and Gratifications

READING:
Elihu Katz, Michael Gurevitch, and Hadassah Hass. "On the Use of the Mass Media for Important Things." *American Sociological Review* 38(1973):164-81.

"Uses and gratifications" is the area of theory that encompasses a wide range of ideas about and inquiries into why and how people use the mass media. Instead of asking what the media do *to* people (as the long history of media-effects studies reveals), uses-and-gratifications researchers ask what people do *with* the mass media. The assumption is that people have needs and desires they can meet by using the media. Of course, not all such needs are articulated or even consciously recognized, but the uses-and-gratifications approach assumes that audience members do select among media and messages and that the selection satisfies a personal drive.

The obvious value of uses-and-gratifications theory is that if audience needs could be identified, the media could better satisfy those needs. But the research has shown there is nothing simple in identifying people's needs.

Researchers have found that people have trouble expressing what needs are served by mass media. If you ask someone why they watch television, they are likely to say, "I watch TV because I like the shows." The response is accurate but does not get at the underlying motivation. (We assume that there is an underlying motivation.) Many respondents haven't given the question much thought, so they can't readily catalogue what expectations are being met through their media use.

People usually use the media for a variety of reasons, not just one. For example, a person reads about political campaigns to learn about the candidates and to prepare to vote but also to learn about threatening issues, changes that affect lifestyle, or other changes that may be forthcoming. Furthermore, a person can hardly avoid the political campaign if one uses media, so some use (and some learning) is purely incidental. Also, the person is likely to discuss the election with friends and family, so they will keep up with the news to be able to provide informed comment. Which, if any, of these reasons for attending to the campaign through the media is paramount?

Researchers have found that people tend to give "expected" reasons for using media. Interviewees are likely to respond with surveillance-type answers such as "to keep up with news events," yet further probing shows they are unable to name any news events they want to keep up with.

Uses-and-gratifications research has also attempted to determine whether gratifications are media-specific. Some studies have shown that print media are used for information, while broadcast media are used for entertainment. Other studies have shown that both types of media are used in a variety of ways, which (in overview) discounts media-specific gratifications.

Although uses-and-gratifications research is sometimes criticized as atheoretical, common sense and personal experience suggest that people seek some gratifications through media use. The following exercise will attempt to show in class just how pervasive the gratifications idea is.

EXERCISE

Consider your own mass media use and complete the sections that follow with reasons why you attend each of the listed media when you do use them. Instead of just reporting that you listen to radio for "music," however, list in your own words the gratifications you get from the music you listen to. Try to take the same broad approach with the other media listed as well.

Newspapers:
(Example: I read the paper for security to be assured the world is still safe.)

Television:

Radio:

Movies:

Magazines:

Records:

Books:

When you have completed your review, look it over to determine if you have any duplication under a single medium (it is certainly possible to list the same gratification for more than one medium.)

Your instructor will take over from this point to compile a list of gratifications the class has named. The instructor may wish to list each separate gratification (reason for using media) on the board and/or to identify the most frequent gratifications named by class members.

UNIT 22
Socialization

READING:
Warren Breed. "Social Control in the Newsroom." *Social Forces* 33(1955):326-35.

Steven H. Chaffee, L. S. Ward, and Leonard P. Tipton. "Mass Communication and Political Socialization." *Journalism Quarterly* 47(1970):647-59.

Like the person who "can't see the forest for the trees," we often look at behavior without considering the process of socialization. We should pause for a moment to consider what life would be like without a social order. Beholden to no one, driven only by survival instincts, we would take our gratifications wherever and whenever circumstances permitted. Ours would not be a pretty scene. It would not be social; it would be downright unsocial.

Fortunately, somewhere along the path of history, we learned that we could maximize our gratifications by not always acting singly; we found strength in numbers and learned that a team was sometimes more effective than a solo effort. Over the ages, we refined the techniques of togetherness until today the rules we live by are themselves a kind of forest, impenetrable and deep. The rules often are subtle and extend to all behaviors. For example, we try hard not to offend someone, even if what we say is true (Smidley may be slovenly and impertinent, but that's for *him* to work out), unless a behavior crosses a certain line. Another example: We restrict our costumes and their colors to certain hours or occasions (no loud colors at a funeral; black tie formal after 6 P.M., etc.), and we show deference in myriad ways. Most of us are highly skilled in these rules of social order, even though the rules are not neatly and plainly written for us to follow.

And that raises the questions: If the rules are not carefully written so that they can be accurately applied, how do we learn them? How are they transmitted from one generation to the next? And who are the teachers?

We learn the elements of social order through a process called socialization. This is a potent term because it implies a basis for all our social and political behavior. A cynic once defined socialization as "how a person gets beaten into the system"; in other words, the person learns to conform, or else. Socialization can be as simple as the casual observation that most people don't talk in elevators (therefore, talking in elevators is not appropriate behavior), and it can be as direct as the modeling of one's behavior after that of a friend or relative.

Some of our social rules *are* written; for example, our legal codes support the social order. Most other social rules are unwritten and dynamic, ebbing and flowing with the prevailing wisdom of the day.

But again, how do we learn? This is important because we need to understand the process. There are policy implications: if we learn from TV and don't like the behavior that is modeled, should we regulate the model?

Learning theory has it that we learn by association, either through classical conditioning or instrumental conditioning. That is, we learn by the pairing of the thing learned with some kind of gratification. By extension, we can say that people learn from media, and they learn best under conditions of association. That includes the idea of "modeling." For instance, suppose we see a movie hero in a daring feat (for example, spinning a red Porsche convertible in the road to avoid a police roadblock); the pairing of the hero with the behavior might make the behavior more acceptable to us.

But, of course, we don't model all that we see; we don't become bank robbers or whatever just because Butch and Sundance had a good time in their western saga. But then again, maybe some of us do. We do learn some things from role models; for instance, many of us vote for one political party because of family tradition, or we purchase one brand of automobile because it served us well in the past.

So there you have a key question: Is social learning (modeling) from media models responsible for a portion of lawbreaking observed in our society? It is obvious that most of us, under most conditions, would not perform deviant behaviors just because they are seen in action drama; but is it possible that some of us, under some conditions (arousal, frustration, lack of an appropriate model), mistakenly adopt a deviant media model?

In its simplest form, social learning theory has it that modeling occurs as a function of attention to the model, retention of the image, ability to emulate the model, and motivation to perform the behavior as well as the functional value of the behavior and the personal characteristics and history of the observer. It is a complex theory that says in effect that some people under some conditions will perform some observed behaviors.[1]

Much of the previous discussion has couched social learning (socialization) in terms of dysfunction. But if we can learn "bad" things from the media, can't we also learn "good" things? Constructive learning is called "prosocial" learning. There is some evidence that children learn useful things from media. For instance, youngsters may develop increased knowledge of public affairs, and surely media also contribute to language skills and social awareness.

---

1. For a detailed examination of the theory, see Albert Bandura, *Social Learning Theory* (Englewood Cliffs, N.J.: Prentice-Hall, 1977).

There is some concern that what children learn from media (especially TV, although in years past the culprit was the comic book) creates an unreal view of life. In a widely reported criminal case, a Florida lad was defended on the basis of supposed addiction to television. The defense was to the effect that the defendant behaved in a bizarre way because he lost his moorings in the unreality of TV. We hope few of us are so addicted, yet there may be a problem; we have referred to it in Unit 20 as the matter of cultivation. The cultivation hypothesis supposes that television shapes a person's world view and that may or may not be functional. It seems that, when our entertainment leans heavily to violent action-drama, many of us, especially those with limited outside contacts, may conclude that life is decidedly harsher and less safe than it really is.

Finally, there is the matter of political socialization, the primary agents of which are the family, the school, one's peer group, and the media. Peculiarly, the latter variable (media) has only been studied fairly recently. If the political news typically involves stories such as "Congressman Jones blasted his opponent today . . ." or "city council lapsed into bedlam today when . . .", then what is a reader likely to learn? Unfortunately, the answer may be cynicism, alienation, disrespect, and belligerence. Chances are that you personally are not conscious of such feelings or you may not have them. But is there, for too many others, a general pervasive distrust of the political system? Is the feeling justified? Is the feeling due in any part to media coverage?

In raising that point, we do not want to seem to attack the press, and we do not favor restriction or censorship. We simply raise the point so that we can consider the issue directly.

EXERCISES

Part A. Identify a political figure whom you admire, preferably one not known to you personally but known to you through the media or other avenue. Try to reconstruct how you came to admire the person.

1. Is the person of the same political persuasion or party as all or most members of your family?

2. Is the person of the same political party or persuasion as yourself?

3. What qualities of this person do you particularly admire?

4. Others might like the same person but for different reasons. Why do you think you emphasized the qualities that you did?

5. Let's say that your political affiliation (Democrat, Republican, Independent, other) indicates your political philosophy. How did you happen to develop that philosophy? Consider the role of the following:
    a. School. Did your teachers, textbooks, or any aspect of the institution play a large role in how you came to view politics?

b. Friends. Would you say your friends (from the time youngsters become politically aware, say, 5th to 6th grade onward) were politically knowledgeable? Largely apathetic? Might they have played a role in your philosophical development?

c. Parents, siblings. Were political affairs discussed in your home? Were you encouraged to participate in discussions? Did discussions proceed from an underlying assumption that politicians were more or less inherently "good" or "bad"? Do not feel obliged to divulge sensitive personal or political experiences other than in general terms.

d. Media--newspapers, radio, TV. What were your political media experiences? Was there particular interest in politics in your home? Did the family very frequently watch the evening news? Read newspapers daily? At what age did you begin to read public affairs in the newspaper?

e. Other. Perhaps there were other sources of political socialization for you; they might have included social clubs, experiences (such as observing a nasty strike or political demonstration), military service, etc. Can you think of instances that made strong impressions on you?

Each of us has a point of view that is built on what we see, learn, and experience. Our point of view is the culmination of the process of socialization, which takes place over a lifetime. In this exercise, we have asked you to indicate "where you are" (re politics), so to speak, and then "how you got there." Your answers are a kind of map of your own political socialization.

Part B. Now let's look at nonpolitical socialization. Reflect on each of the following questions and write a brief response.

1. Who were some of the significant social influences in your childhood years, ages 3 through 12? (For example, did you spend most of your time away from school with a sitter, at a day-care center, with a parent, with a substitute parent such as a relative? Presumably, a lot of your early training was due to that person or persons.)

2. Who were some of the significant social influences in your teenage years? (Might be parents, relatives, peers, teachers, church, etc.)

3. What are some of your favorite pastimes or activities today, and how did you happen to develop them? (Example, you like to sew, draw, or work on cars; how did you get "into" that?)

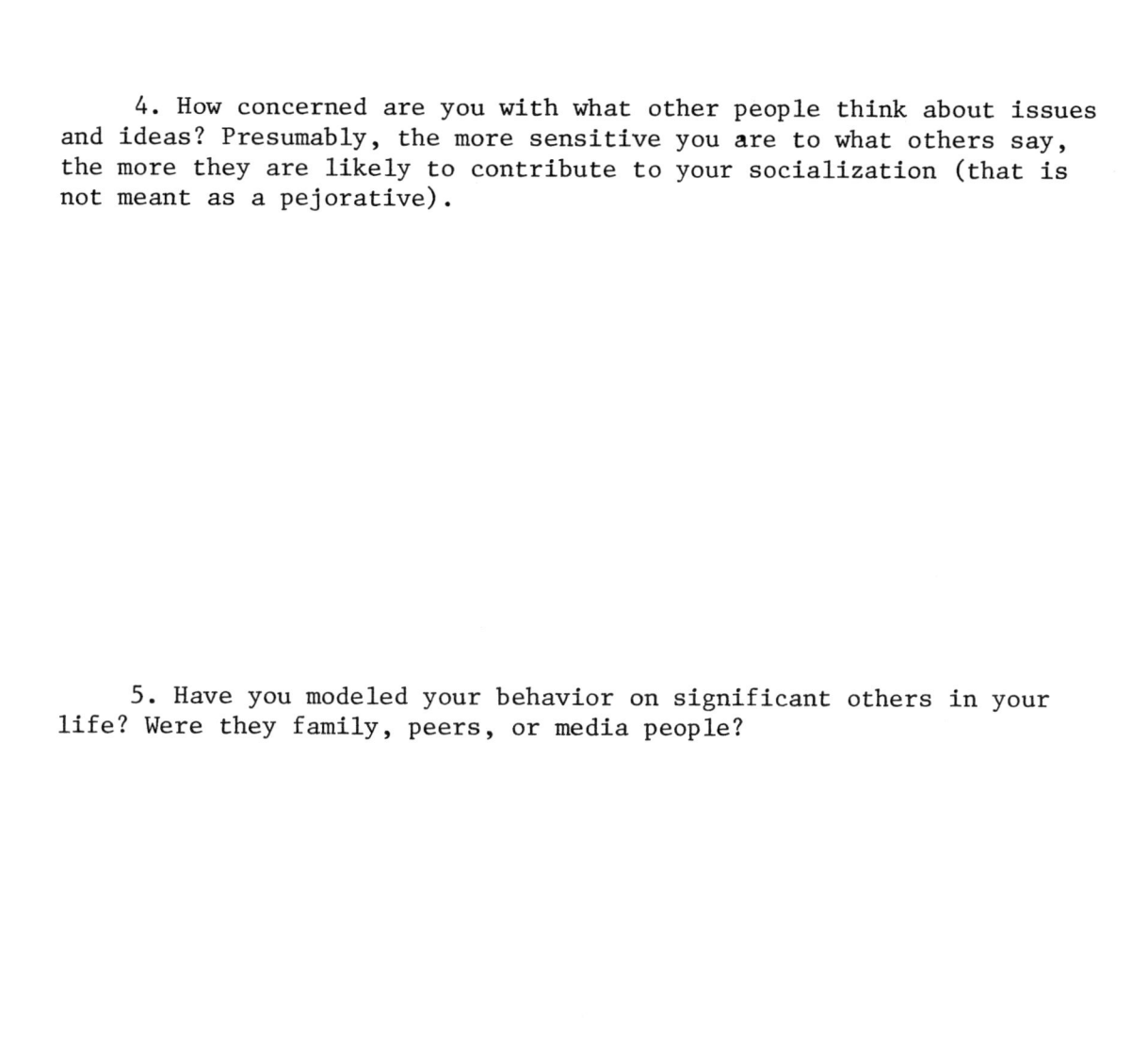

4. How concerned are you with what other people think about issues and ideas? Presumably, the more sensitive you are to what others say, the more they are likely to contribute to your socialization (that is not meant as a pejorative).

5. Have you modeled your behavior on significant others in your life? Were they family, peers, or media people?

6. What are your own thoughts on modeling, socialization, political socialization? (Are we giving TV too much credit for teaching and the individual too little credit for good judgment?)

UNIT 23
Coorientation

READING:
Steven H. Chaffee and Jack M. McLeod. "Sensitization in Panel Design: A Coorientation Experiment." *Journalism Quarterly* 45 (1968):661-90.

Daniel B. Wackman. "Interpersonal Communication and Coorientation." *American Behavioral Scientist* 16(1973):537-50.

Chaffee and McLeod introduced the concept "coorientation" in the late 1960s. Coorientation has to do principally with simultaneous orientation to concepts, objects, or persons. Most previous research dealt with effects of media on people, especially persuasion effects. Chaffee and McLeod's concept suggested that, logically enough, if Person A were to persuade Person B, then Person B would have to first understand the communication. Understanding should be greatest when the orientation of A and B to the object of communication is closest. For example, if you wanted to convince a young person to avoid non-prescription drugs, what kind of persuader would you seek? A business-suited person who had only secondary knowledge of drugs? Or a street-wise person who spoke "the same language" as the listener? Presumably, for this topic, you would pick the latter. But does that mean the cooriented peer will always make the best presenter? No. Undoubtedly, it would depend on the topic, the presenter, the listener, and probably a host of other variables. The study of coorientation is the search for a systematic relationship among the relevant variables.

EXERCISE

Below are 10 assertions about conditions, opportunities, and practices in your area. Review each assertion carefully and decide whether (or to what extent) you agree or disagree with the assertion. On the form that follows, indicate your agreement or disagreement.

1. Local auto drivers are careful, considerate, and cautious.
2. Parking spaces are extremely difficult to locate on this campus.

The authors wish to thank Professor Ann Landini for assisting in development of the exercise in this unit.

3. An abundance of excellent restaurants can be found locally if one would just look.
4. The climate here is "moderate."
5. Our undergraduate students represent a diverse geographic and cultural mix.
6. Merchants here welcome business from undergraduate and graduate students.
7. Local TV news is highly professional.
8. Local newspapers emphasize in-depth reporting of local events.
9. Our library system makes it easy for students to find books and other instructional materials.
10. Adequate cultural activities are provided for our students.

On the form below, indicate agreement/disagreement with each of the previously given assertions.

Code: SA = strongly agree, A = agree, NO = no opinion, D = disagree, SD = strongly disagree.

1. ___ ___ ___ ___ ___
   SA   A   NO   D   SD

2. ___ ___ ___ ___ ___
   SA   A   NO   D   SD

3. ___ ___ ___ ___ ___
   SA   A   NO   D   SD

4. ___ ___ ___ ___ ___
   SA   A   NO   D   SD

5. ___ ___ ___ ___ ___
   SA   A   NO   D   SD

6. ___ ___ ___ ___ ___
   SA   A   NO   D   SD

7. ___ ___ ___ ___ ___
   SA   A   NO   D   SD

8. ___ ___ ___ ___ ___
   SA   A   NO   D   SD

9. ___ ___ ___ ___ ___
   SA   A   NO   D   SD

10. ___ ___ ___ ___ ___
    SA   A   NO   D   SD

Analysis of responses can be in the form of hypothesis testing or simple anecdote. Suggestions for statistical analysis are given in the Instructor's Manual.

At the discretion of the instructor, each class member should identify another class member not very well known to him or her and compare agreement for the 10 assertions. If differences are found, the two should attempt to learn the reasons for them.

Discussion should include knowledge of the following elements important to the concept of coorientation:

1. *Congruence* is the similarity between one person's cognitions and those he or she attributes to another person. (For greater detail, refer to the suggested reading.)

2. *Agreement* is the extent to which persons A and B attach the same importance to the object; especially, agreement on the attributes of the object.

3. *Accuracy* is the degree of matching (actual, rather than perceived) between what A and B think.

As you discuss agreement or disagreement on an assertion, can you determine whether it was a function of congruence, agreement, or accuracy?

Can you trace other sources of differing perceptions toward the assertions?

In the space below, discuss briefly the kinds of differences you found and the likely reasons for them. Continue on an extra sheet of paper if needed.

UNIT 24
Nonhuman Communication

READING:
Melvin De Fleur and Sandra Ball-Rokeach. *Theories of Mass Communication*, 3d ed. New York: David McKay, 1975, pp. 108-20.

Humans are fascinated with nonhuman communication. The idea that our household pets and the tiniest insects communicate makes us wonder about what levels of thinking nonhuman species actually have.

EXERCISE

Here is a simple exercise that includes a little library work but should be well worth the effort.

1. Go to the university library reference section and find the card catalogue subject area. Look up "animal" and then find "communication."
2. Choose one of the books on a topic that appeals to you and locate it in the library.
3. Read enough of the book to be able to complete the animal communication assignment on the following page (to be turned in at the beginning of the next class meeting).
4. The Believe It or Not section must include a single "astounding" fact about some aspect of animal (fish, fowl, insect, reptile, mammal) communication. It can be as short as a single sentence or as long as a paragraph.
5. Be sure to complete every line of the source citation at the bottom of the assignment sheet.

This assignment should take no more than an hour of out-of-class time to complete, unless you find you can't put the library book down.

ANIMAL COMMUNICATION ASSIGNMENT

Name:_____

Date:_____

Class:_____

Believe It or Not!

Source:

Full name of book:_____

Full name of author(s):_____

Publisher:_____ Publication city:_____

Publication state:_____ Date of publication:_____

Pages on which fact is found:_____ to_____

UNIT 25
Prosocial and Antisocial Learning

READING:
Alexis Tan. "Prosocial Effects of Television." *Mass Communication Theories and Research*, 2d ed. Wiley: New York, 1985, pp. 287-98.

It was suggested in Unit 22 that media effects can be either prosocial or antisocial. That is, we are exposed to media content that we would judge as making either a positive or negative contribution to social behavior if acted out by the individual. If we observe a good Samaritan helping a fellow in distress, we might call that action prosocial because it would contribute to social well-being. Conversely, if we observe the Samaritan being robbed, we judge that to be antisocial.

People who watch television see incidents of antisocial behavior presented as "entertainment." Studies have shown that TV murders number in four figures during the course of a year. The sum of all acts of TV violence is huge. How often do we see prosocial acts on TV? We will try to find out when we do the brief study below. And as you read the remainder of this discussion and as you do the exercise, ask yourself the questions: What is being "learned" from TV? Only the prosocial? What is meant by "learned"? What is the social implication of a heavy national entertainment diet of mayhem?

PROSOCIAL LEARNING

Tan reviewed numerous studies of the prosocial effects of children's programs such as "Mister Rogers's Neighborhood" and "Sesame Street." He concluded that "there is considerable evidence that children can and do learn from television." He said the learning can be cognitive, helping children ages three to five prepare for school. Prosocial learning also can be effective, "beneficial to ourselves and others." For example, children can learn attitudes related to racial harmony or occupational opportunity. Tan said some children can generalize what they learn to other behavioral contexts. So we have it that children learn prosocial information from TV. Presumably, they learn it because the knowledge is reinforced in some positive way. It does not appear that they learn equal amounts of antisocial information. Presumably, this is because of negative reinforcement; parents tell their children not to behave that way. But now another tough question: What happens in the absence of negative reinforcement? Might a child left to his or her own devices (that is, unsupervised) in front of a TV learn more antisocial behavior than one carefully supervised?

ANTISOCIAL LEARNING

Research on antisocial effects of TV has been voluminous and controversial. The studies number in the high hundreds, and the dollar cost is in the millions. Not all the studies support the premise of antisocial learning, and some use controversial data-gathering techniques. What, then, should we make of the data? We might liken the situation to the criterion in a criminal trial: Is TV guilty of antisocial instruction beyond a reasonable doubt? If a jury was asked to decide, you would probably see a hung jury. But if you used the civil court standard, the preponderance of evidence, the court just might rule in favor of the complainant. It seems that more and more researchers are concluding that there is a positive relationship between exposure to aggression and subsequent violent behavior, at least among predisposed individuals.

While a stronger conclusion (one with less equivocation) might be ardently desired, social research methods (given ethical constraints) just don't seem to be able to answer the questions clearly. Researchers are not permitted to intrude into people's lives; they cannot get into their audiences' head; and in the absence of sufficient data, the suspicion that TV violence is related to public misbehavior is stronger than the available data show.

EXERCISES

Part A. Let's say our research techniques are inadequate, and in place of research let's use reason and intuition. After all, whoever said truth was limited to a random sample, a Solomon four-way research design, or a complex statistical hypothesis test? Try your intuition on the following:

1. People watch TV, and they learn from TV. Therefore, in general, the more TV that is watched, the more that is learned.
2. What is learned (observed and recalled) becomes data for interpretation of subsequent information.
3. Therefore, heavy viewers embody more of a "TV reality" than light viewers.
4. The direction of what is learned can be positive, negative, or neutral (that is, prosocial, antisocial, or neutral).
5. What is learned becomes part of the basis for behavior.

What are your own thoughts on this? Does your own intuition, your own evaluation, lead to the same "logical" structure as above? If not, build your own scenario. Use the space below to reflect on these questions and to address the issues yourself.

Part B. The discussion sets up an interesting exercise. If TV programs include prosocial and antisocial acts, with what frequency do these acts occur? And do they occur with equal frequency? Let's do a little counting.

    1. Select any two-hour block of prime-time TV programming on either of the three major entertainment networks.
    2. Observe the programs for the two-hour period and record the number of prosocial and antisocial acts you see.
    3. Define your terms.

        Example: Prosocial is any behavior that contributes favorably to social order.
        Example: Prosocial is any instance of one person helping another.

(Make your definitions as clear as possible so that another person would be able to come behind you and get the same counts.)
    4. Do a brief pilot test; that is, before you begin your two-hour study, start with a brief segment of programming that will allow you to estimate whether your definitions will work. If possible, improve your definitions based on the pilot test.
    5. Watch the two hours of prime-time TV and count each instance of prosocial or antisocial behavior. Try to make notes about each instance so that you will be able to recall them and discuss them in class.

6. List the number of prosocial and antisocial acts on the form that follows and discuss in the spaces provided below the form.

Prosocial	Antisocial
1.	1.
2.	2.
3.	3.
4.	4.
5.	5.
6.	6.
7.	7.
8.	8.
9.	9.
10.	10.
11.	11.
12.	12.
13.	13.
14.	14.
15.	15.

What problems did you encounter in doing this exercise? What can you conclude based on your data? Discuss.

If another person applied your definitions, would they get the same results? Discuss.

UNIT 26

Spiral of Silence

READING:
Carrol J. Glynn and Jack M. McLeod. "Implications of the Spiral of Silence Theory for Communication and Public Opinion Research." *Communication Yearbook* (International Communication Association), 1982.

Elisabeth Noelle-Neumann. "The Spiral of Silence: A Theory of Public Opinion." *Journal of Communication* 24(1974):449-58.

Noelle-Neumann, a West German researcher, developed an intriguing theory of public opinion. A professor of communication research at the University of Mainz, Noelle-Neumann was especially interested in the process by which public opinion is formed. Her research indicated that individuals were influenced not only by what others said but by what the individuals expected others would say. She suggested that if an individual expected his or her opinion would be in a minority or would be received with disdain, the person was less likely to speak up. People who anticipated support for their position and who then spoke out were, in effect, reinforced in their behavior. They became stronger while the others became weaker; hence, the "spiral of silence."

The theory has several points, but one of special interest is the perception of what "others" think. Noelle-Neumann suggested that individuals use a quasi-statistical approach, in the sense that individuals might estimate the frequency of support for a line of thought. In some regards, the idea makes good sense. After all, who among us would like to volunteer, "I appreciated the service of Vice President Agnew," when probably most others (who know of his political and legal difficulties) in the group would disagree? Put yourself in that position: would you be likely to volunteer an unpopular position? Clearly, some will state their feelings in the face of opposition; others will not.

Noelle-Neumann explained that our reluctance to take an unpopular position is based on our fear of isolation. "To the individual, not isolating himself is more important than his non-judgment. This appears to be a condition of life in human society; if it were otherwise, sufficient integration could not be achieved," she said. Have you seen an example of this? Is it really fear of isolation that moves a person to silence? Does it depend on issue strength, the urgency of the solution, or something else?

Noelle-Neumann said it is not only fear of isolation but doubt about one's capacity for judgment that makes the individual vulnerable, and one's social groups can "punish him for failing to toe the line." She said public opinion, sanction, and punishment were closely linked.

The "spiral of silence" is an interesting idea and an important contribution; yet its acceptance has not been complete. For example, Glynn and McLeod said the idea was open to criticism on both theoretical and methodological grounds and that Noelle-Neumann's concepts were not always clearly explained and some were never studied. Glynn and McLeod used data from U.S. elections to test the theory, and they found only partial support. They added, however, that it was obvious the idea held important implications and said definitional entanglements should be worked out.

Granted, this description of the theory has been brief; it is assumed the student will use the assigned or other readings to fill in the details.

EXERCISE

Identify and record below a topic of considerable controversy and importance. The controversy can be proximal or distant but preferably one that is "emerging," not "tired." (Examples: government-supported abortion, separation of church and state, deployment of the latest defense system.)

Assuming the controversy can be put in an agree-disagree context, give your best estimate of the percent of students in your class (or school) who feel as you do on the issue. _____%

Is your own position on the presumed *majority* side or in the *minority*?

Now imagine the following: you are in a casual group of 10 of your classmates, and the discussion is generally light; then a controversial issue is broached, but without favor or disfavor. How likely are you, after estimating the level of support for your position, to speak your mind on the issue?

extremely likely_____   somewhat unlikely_____

somewhat likely_____   extremely unlikely_____

If your position is in the minority, would you feel "isolated"?

Write your comments below as to the accuracy and usefulness of the "spiral of silence" to the understanding of public opinion.

If a person is unwilling to speak out, could it be because of something positive rather than negative (fear of isolation)? For example, could it be that the speaker simply does not want to offend a listener? Or if a person does speak up, could it be due to a need for, say, dominance?

PART THREE

Some Research Methods in Communication Theory

UNIT 27
Knowing Research Terms

READING:
Earl R. Babbie. *The Practice of Social Research*, 2d ed. Belmont, Calif.: Wadsworth, 1979.

Philip Emmert and William D. Brooks, eds. *Methods of Research in Communication*. Boston: Houghton Mifflin, 1970.

Fred N. Kerlinger. *Foundations of Behavioral Research*. New York: Holt, Rinehart, and Winston, 1973.

Each professional field has its jargon, the words peculiar to the field and laden with meaning. Several terms important to social research are given below. Students are asked to use whatever library resources are necessary to provide definitions of terms and examples illustrating each. The intent of the exercise is direct: if the student is required to conceptualize situations involving the terms, the meanings may be more quickly and permanently internalized.

EXERCISE

Here is an example of how to proceed:

1. Significance. Example: Let's say two groups were compared. The mean of group 1 was 3.51, and the mean of group 2 was 4.68. In a statistical test (say, t-test), the difference was significant at the .05 level. That means a difference that large would occur by chance only 5 times in 100.
2. Internal validity. Example:

3. External validity. Example:

4. Reliability. Example:

5. Sampling frame. Example:

6. Sampling error. Example:

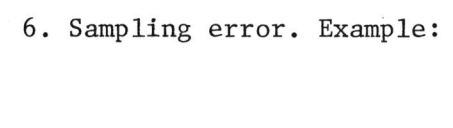

7. Research hypothesis. Example:

8. Null hypothesis. Example:

9. Experimental control. Example:

10. Experimental manipulation. Example:

11. Content analysis. Example:

12. Operational definition. Example:

13. Correlation. Example:

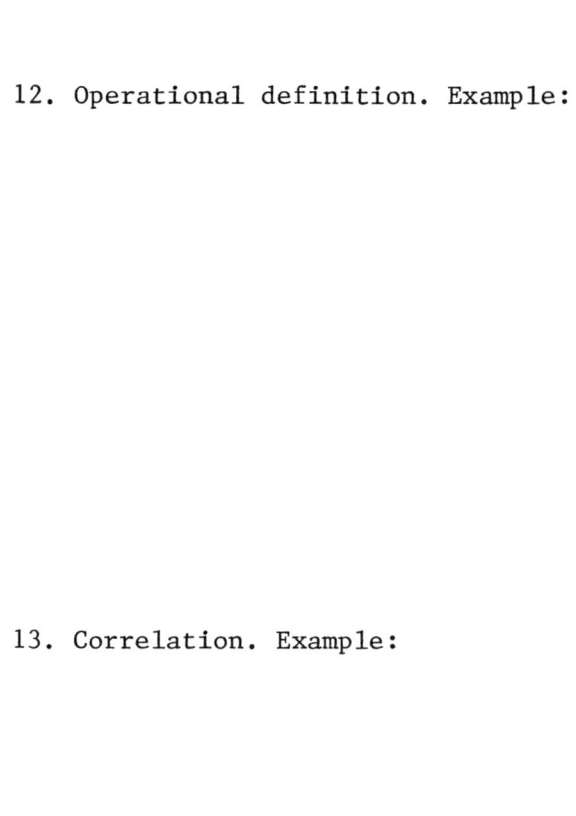

14. Dependent variable. Example:

15. Independent variable. Example:

16. Random sample. Example:

17. Intervening variable. Example:

18. Chi-square, or contingency analysis. Example:

19. Pre-post test. Example:

UNIT 28
Critiquing the Data of Theory

READING:
R. B. Rubin, A. M. Rubin, and L. J. Piele. *Communication Research: Strategies and Sources*. Belmont, Calif.: Wadsworth, 1986, pp. 155-69.

Although theories sometimes are generated through idle speculation, the most useful theories today (and the most intricate) are based on data generated through social science research.

If the student of theory is to appreciate the extent to which a theory or hypothesis is supported by data, the student must become familiar with the format, style, and some of the terms of communication research publications.

Following are some of the primary journals in which communication research is published: *Journalism Quarterly, Journal of Broadcasting, Journal of Communication, Public Opinion Quarterly, Newspaper Research Journal, Human Communication Research, Communication Research, Journal of Advertising, Journal of Advertising Research, Gazette, Journal of Communication Management, Journal of Consumer Research, Journalism History, Journalism Monographs, Public Relations Quarterly, Public Relations Journal*. (Other important journals are found in the fields of psychology, sociology, government, and elsewhere.)

Research reports in the form of journal articles typically have some or all of the following parts: introduction, statement of the problem, literature review, research methods, results and analysis, and conclusions or summary. Other points to look for are formal or working hypotheses, internal/external validity, reliability, method of statistical analysis (including sampling frame, sample size, sampling error, significance level), support or nonsupport for hypotheses.

The *introduction* is the stage setter, the statement that expresses the conditions leading to the need for research. The introduction may be only a few lines, or several pages. The introduction usually includes a *statement of the problem*, covering the need for research. A *literature review* includes relevant data or observations from any source; the review should be exhaustive. The literature review brings the reader up to date on what is known about the topic and may lead directly to a *statement of hypothesis*. In other words, a review of previous research may lead the researcher to hypothesize thus and so. The formal hypothesis is most often either logical (if A and B, then C) or comparative (A does not equal B, or A is related to B).

The section on *research methods* simply explains how the data are to be gathered and analyzed. Research methods should also include information on the *method of statistical analysis*, that is, on the *sampling frame* (the population from which the sample is drawn), *sample size* (the number of elements purporting to represent the population) and how the sample is to be drawn. *Sampling error* refers to the extent to which the sample may deviate from the mean of the "true" population, if the true mean was known. Knowledge of statistics is more or less required for critical review of modern social science research. However, the layperson can look for level of *statistical significance*, that is, the probability that such a difference in scores would occur by chance alone. Significance is usually set at the .05, .01, or .001 level and may be interpreted thus: only five times in a hundred (or, say, one in a thousand) would a difference as large as that observed occur as a function of random variation. In other words, significance at .05 or below means a difference is unlikely to occur merely by chance; hence the difference must be attributable to something else, presumably the element under study.

We may think of social science research as the business of establishing objective truth, the gathering of statements of substance that scholars can agree upon. That being the goal, the *results* section of any research article should be presented with great care and caution. You may find it necessary to review the research method, the sample, and the statistical analysis and estimate whether the data do indeed suggest the certainty or uncertainty indicated by the author. Finally, you may agree or disagree with the author's *conclusions*. (In some articles, the conclusions section is replaced by a *summary*.)

When you consider the appropriateness of the research sample, the key is *validity*. In lay terms, internal validity refers to the extent to which the research "measured what it was supposed to measure." For instance, if a researcher wished to measure attitude toward something but had a poor measure of attitude, the study would lack internal validity. External validity refers to the extent to which a research situation may be generalized to a larger population. For example, if the research sample is a group of 40 freshmen, can we say their behavior represents all people, all freshmen, or all campus (local) freshmen, etc.? *Reliability* refers to the extent to which repeated measures yield the same results.

Finally, you should be aware that a single research project never "proves" or "disproves" anything; rather, we say the data "support" or "do not support" the hypothesis. In a manner of speaking, we may consider individual research projects as similar to the bricks in a wall; an isolated brick, or even a good scattering of bricks, does not resemble a wall, but if enough bricks (projects) are accumulated on the project, then an outline may begin to form. If the outline becomes clear enough, we may synthesize the data into a theory, principle, or even a "law." But if the outline is to be clear, the elements within must be firm. The goal of the following exercise is to judge the merits of supposed evidence on important social topics.

EXERCISE

On the opening page of this unit, several journals in communication research were named. Review one or more of those journals to identify an article of interest. Then read the article carefully and evaluate it, applying the following criteria:

1. Identify author and give full citation.

2. Introduction. Describe the introduction as to length, clarity, separation from literature review (is there any separation?), whether it includes a statement of the problem (either by formal statement or by implication), and/or any other characteristic you observe.

3. Literature review. Describe the literature review. Is it persuasive by its depth, clarity, and logical presentation? Does the research question or hypothesis flow from the findings of previous research?

4. Hypothesis, research problem. If the hypothesis or research problem is formally stated, write it below. If it is only implied, give your description of the working hypothesis. If formally stated, is the hypothesis of the logical type or the comparative type?

5. Research methods. Describe the sample and its suitability for the proposed research. Comment on internal and external validity. Identify significance level. Are the methods suited to the problem?

6. Results and conclusions. In your judgment, to what extent were the data confirmatory or not? Did the research persuasively answer a research question? Where is the research likely to go from here? Did you identify research questions you might be interested in looking into?

UNIT 29
The .05 Level of Significance

READING:
Sanford Labovitz. "Criteria for Selecting a Significance Level: A Note on the Sacredness of .05." *American Sociologist* 3(August 1968):220-22.

We learn that the .05 level is the accepted level of significance for all social science research, and only those who are well into the study of statistics ever question why. Labovitz (and others) makes a case for occasionally setting other levels, and we look at some of this rationale after pausing to review what a significance level is.

Sometimes called a "confidence" or "probability" level, the *significance level* is set by the researcher doing the study and means there is a level at which the findings from the study could be chance findings. The .05 level means that five times out of 100 possible repetitions of the study the findings should not be believed because they could have occurred by chance. The findings could be believed in 95 of the 100 possible repetitions, which is pretty good odds. However, we never know which of the 100 possible outcomes this finding represents. The .01 level means a finding could be based on chance only one time out of 100 possible repetitions. Since no one is going to repeat the study 100 times, the significance level is really saying there is a 5% or a 1% chance that the findings being reported aren't to be believed.

Naturally, every researcher would like to be able to say the findings being reported are absolute, that they can be believed 100% of the time, particularly those findings the researcher is currently reporting. But absolute confidence in any result based on a random sample is impossible. Still, five times to err out of 100 is not too bad; one time out of 100 is much better and one time out of 1,000 (the .001 level) is very much better.

The greater the confidence needed, the stricter the researcher must be. If the researcher requires the results of a study to be reliable 99 times out of 100 possible tests, the confidence level must be .01. Nobody wants to make the error of reporting an important research finding that may only represent chance. But if the significance level is strict enough (.001) to assure the finding is real, we run the risk of never having any important findings to report. A researcher who sets significance at too strict a level (.001) may make the error of not reporting a real finding that should be reported and will fail to support a theory that should be supported. The researcher who sets the significance level too low (.10) will occasionally support theory for which no support is deserved.

So the problem of setting a significance level is a double-edged sword that can injure not only the researcher but also the observer, the person who reads research reports and tries to evaluate their worth. Hence a presentation of some considerations needed to assess a significance level follows:

1. Consequence of reaching erroneous conclusions. Social scientists often deal with research topics that might further knowledge but may mar their reputations if they are later found in error. For instance, an erroneous conclusion that radio drama is more involving for listeners than television drama is for viewers may result in a producer losing money. The researcher's erroneous report, based on a .05 significance level, would do little harm. On the other hand, a researcher may erroneously conclude that presenting videotaped testimony to juries results in the same verdicts the juries would have reached with testimony presented in court from the witness stand. This conclusion may be responsible for the prison term of the defendant or worse. Such a conclusion should be based on research that has withstood a rigorous test. In cases where an error may have grievous results, the .01 or .001 significance level should be used.

2. Sample size. Virtually every statistical test is sensitive to sample size, since sample size is part of the test's formula. A large sample will produce significant differences even when the percentage of actual difference in the dependent measures is very small; a sample of 4,800 cases may yield a statistically significant difference at the .05 level when one group scores an 86 on a 100-point test while the other scores an 83. On the other hand, a very small sample yields statistically significant differences only when the actual differences noted are great. On the 100-point test, with a sample of only 50 cases, one group's score of 66 might not be considered statistically different from another group's score of 86. With very large samples, the significance level should be more strict, say .01 or .001; with very small samples, a significance level of .05 or .10 might be the better choice.

3. Extent of past research. In studies based on evidence that has already been tested and reported, the significance level should be more stringent, at the .01 level or the .001 level. Here the previous research has provided insights and built a case for accepting one position or the other. (In some instances, even a lot of previous work may leave the position in doubt because much of the research might have reached conflicting conclusions.) But in any event, the more a researcher has to go on, the more stringently the significance level should be set for the current study. If the current study's outcome conflicts with past research, its report should be based on test conclusions in which the researcher and report reader will have confidence. Also, if the new study supports the position that past research has established, it should be able to do so after passing hurdles as rigorous as those of its predecessors.

4. Control in research design. A well-controlled design (one that accounts for most of the possible intervening variables) should not require as much rigor in its significance level. On the other hand, a loosely designed test in which several possible intervening variables are discovered should pass a stringent significance level such as .01 or .001 before being reported for acceptance with any confidence by readers.

5. Size of expected outcome differences. If there is reason to expect a large difference in dependent variable outcomes, the significance level should be set at .01 or .001, a more stringent level. Experience and common knowledge tell a researcher that blind people have more developed hearing than sighted people. A hearing test is given to a sample of blind people and a sample of sighted people, and the blind people do show higher scores on hearing sensitivity. However, the difference between the two groups is only significant at the .05 level. Since the researcher expected a more substantial difference in scores, the hypothesis that blind people have more sensitive hearing than sighted people is (perhaps) rejected as a chance finding for this particular study.

6. Strength of the statistical test. Without delving too deeply into statistical testing, we may note that all tests aren't equal. Some require that several assumptions about the sample and distribution of dependent variable scores are met. The extent to which these assumptions are violated should be considered by the researcher, and the more deviance there is from test assumptions, the more stringent the significance level should be (.01 or .001).

One other comment should be made about the strength of the statistical tests used. For example, Spearman's rank correlation coefficient is based on ranks only, while Pearson's product-moment correlation is based on interval data. Although the two statistical tests are different and compensate for the levels of measurement, the researcher might want to base selection of a significance level on knowledge of the two tests. Consider the following set of test scores from subjects A through E:

Subject	Spearman Ranks	Pearson Intervals
A	1	.98
B	2	.91
C	4	.74
D	3	.85
E	5	.62

Without going further in diagnosing the differences between Spearman and Pearson measures, it is obvious the Pearson data are more sophisticated, while the Spearman data are only relative measures (subject C didn't actually score a "4"; the subject was merely in fourth place). Since the Spearman data are less powerful, outcomes based on them should have a more rigorous significance level, say, .01 or .001. The Pearson data are more powerful measures, hence a significance level of .05 may be enough to have faith that a hypothesis has actually been supported.

EXERCISE

Labovitz offers 11 considerations (including those discussed above) about determining the proper significance level, but the others are far beyond the scope of this exercise. Here you are to set the proper significance level for the following research situations and briefly explain which of the six points given above has influenced your decision (some may use two or more):

1. Using census data for New York City, a researcher has concluded that Manhattan residents are wealthier than residents in the other four boroughs.

2. Using factor analysis on a sample of 1,000, a researcher finds people who like one type of television show also name blue as their favorite color.

3. In a sample of 100 people at a fair, 58% pick Pepsi-Cola over Coca-Cola when blindfolded.

4. Results on monkeys over a period of two years indicate a new drug is likely to minimize the ill effects of body chemical rejection in human transplant recipients.

5. Children of police are tested against a sample of 5,000 non-police children to see if the opinion of the two groups on capital punishment differs.

6. A researcher devises a new experiment to determine if violence on television has an adverse effect on children.

7. You are the head of a city utility company and a chemist says he has discovered a much less expensive additive for natural gas so people can be warned of danger if they smell a gas leak.

8. Using a modern greenhouse, controlled lighting, and plant rotation methods, a forester believes he has found a new fertilizer that speeds plant growth.

9. Three classrooms of fifth graders are given a test on the book all have been using as a reader for six weeks. One class's average score is 82, another's is 68, and the third's is 93.

10. A team of researchers watches grocery shoppers in every store one weekend in a city of 300,000 population; 45% of women shoppers use coupons vs. 48% of male shoppers.

UNIT 30
Journal Synopses

READING:
Edward T. Cremmins. *The Art of Abstracting*. Philadelphia: ISI Press, 1982.

Students of theory in mass communication learn early that their work involves the collection and analysis of previous research. Virtually every thesis and dissertation includes a section called "review of literature," which is the presentation of what has been written on the current topic (or closely related topics) by previous researchers and writers.

Not just major works such as theses but virtually every journal article includes a section that can be called a review of literature, which usually comes at the beginning of the article either before or immediately following the problem section or purpose of the study. In terms of its structure, then, a journal article can be seen as a mini-thesis.

Undergraduates and graduate students alike will learn quickly that they are expected to know how to gather and present what is already known about a topic, even in their class papers. The procedure is often accomplished through a journal synopsis, a one-page summary of a journal article that provides enough overview of the information in the article to allow someone who may not have read it to understand what it was all about and what conclusions it reached.

This unit is designed to show you how to do a journal synopsis by following the eight steps below. An example of a completed synopsis paper is then presented. Admittedly, not all journal articles are created equal. Some will not fit well into the format being described, but most of the data-based journal articles do, and you will find ways to bend the format to fit those that do not.

1. The first step is to locate articles that are germane to the topic you are interested in writing about in your own paper. Don't stretch the point too far by including a journal article that only mentions your topic interest in passing. You can often tell by the title of the article or by using a keyword search through an index.

The final point here is not to select a journal article you can't understand. Unfortunately, too many are so loaded with technical jargon that they are unreadable. Or it may be that an article is clearly written, but the level of technical expertise is beyond a beginning student's skills in statistics. If you can't understand it, you won't be able to explain it to someone else.

2. Rely on the subheadings as you read the piece. Generally they will help you place the different subsections of the article into your synopsis format.

3. Avoid repeating the author's jargon. If a subgroup of soap opera viewers are termed "vicarious supplanters," define what that means in your synopsis.

4. Use headings as you jot notes while reading the article. You can probably write your synopsis as you make notes if you categorize as follows: problem, method, findings, evaluation.

5. Use your own words as you write the synopsis. If you rely on the author's way of writing, you may rewrite the article, but you won't be able to boil it down to manageable size.

6. Aim for a one-page, single-spaced sheet as the upper length of your synopsis. You may have to rewrite your synopsis to get it to this length; it is possible that some articles can't be effectively reduced to that extent, but try to keep it succinct while retaining the essence of the article.

7. The beginning citation must be complete. Go over it to ensure that you have presented the full author name(s), full title of the article, full title of the journal, date, volume number, and pages. You should actually get into the habit of doing this first or you will spend needless time returning to the library to verify the citation.

8. The evaluation section is probably the hardest part to do, but it is one of the most important aspects of doing a journal synopsis. This is the part in which you step away from your reading for comprehension and try to assess the merit of the research. What are its strengths and weaknesses? How does this article compare with others on similar topics? After you have completed a few journal synopses, you will find yourself analyzing the value of all articles you review. You will have achieved one goal of every researcher, a healthy skepticism.

EXAMPLE OF A JOURNAL SYNOPSIS REPORT

GATEKEEPING

David M. White. "The Gate Keeper: A Case Study in the Selection of News." *Journalism Quarterly* 41(1951):489-94.

Problem. A news item travels through communication channels run on a system of "gates," each presided over by a "gatekeeper" who controls what happens to it. Each gatekeeper has an incalculable effect on the structure and destiny of every item. What influences may be found to affect the gatekeeper's choice?

Method. The study analyzed the choices of news items made by a wire editor, the final gatekeeper in the news flow chain. He was the most important because his rejection of a story negated all the work of the previous gatekeepers. This wire editor was in his midforties with 25 years experience as a journalist. He was wire editor of a morning paper with about 30,000 circulation in a highly industrialized midwestern city of 100,000.

The gatekeeper who participated in the study stored all rejected wire copy with a notation as to why the story was not used. The amount of news wire copy received was compared with that used, and the reasons for rejection were analyzed.

Findings. Only 10% of the wire copy received was used. The reasons for rejection of 90% were found to be highly subjective. Decisions made were based on value judgments through the gatekeeper's set of experiences, attitudes, and expectations. The gatekeeper cited many reports on the same event, the lack of news value in an item, and limited space as primary reasons for rejection; but the researcher documented that the gatekeeper (1) used stories that interested him and (2) his conception of his public was far from the actual composition of people in his readership audience.

Evaluation. The study states that subjective rather than purely objective news values determine story use, but the study was not well controlled. Would the findings have been the same if a group rather than one wire editor was studied? The study does not build from this single experiment to a broad theory of how mass communication works.

UNIT 31
Sampling, Sampling Distribution, Sampling Error

READING:
Phillip Meyer. *Precision Journalism*. Bloomington: Indiana University Press, 1973.

Julian L. Simon. *Basic Research Methods in Social Science: The Art of Empirical Investigation*, 2d ed. New York: Random House, 1978, pp. 126-44.

Social science research data often are obtained from samples of people whom the researchers expect are representative of some larger population. For example, a survey purporting to represent what 220 million Americans think may be based on only 1,000 to 2,000 interviews or as few as 400. Naturally, the quality of a researcher's conclusions, and the quality of subsequent theories, depends on the quality of the sample as well as the quality of the researchers' interpretation of the data.

What conditions can confound or distort a sample? One is the possibility that not all the elements of a population were given the opportunity to be included. If a researcher is to make an inference from a sample to a population, every element in the population must be given the opportunity to be selected. To the extent that elements are not included, data interpretability is diminished. For instance, suppose you wish to learn what the people of Yourtown feel about issue A, but suppose there is a residual portion of the population that researchers typically cannot reach. Would you learn what they think if you could not ask them? Probably not, so interpretation would become tenuous.

Another problem, and this is what we wish to focus upon, has to do with the *distribution* of the sample. Let's suppose that we know from student records that the average student age on Yourcampus is 22.9 years. But let's say we draw two *samples*, one of 100 persons and one of 300 persons, and that we find the mean (average) for each. Two things probably become very clear: the sample averages are different from the true age of the student population, and the sample averages are different from each other. The larger sample ($n = 300$) was no assurance of accuracy, nor would it be if it was 1,300 instead of 300. If the samples had been carefully drawn, why were they unlike the true mean? The answer has to do with what is known as *sampling distribution* and *sampling error*.

Any time the researcher finds it necessary to use a sample rather than a census, the problem of mean variation (sampling error) occurs.

Sometimes the variation from the "true" (or population) mean is very slight; in other cases it is very great. You can observe for yourself the nature of the problem by beginning the exercise that follows.

EXERCISES

Part A: Selecting a sample. Here are your instructions. With eyes closed, put the point of your pencil gently onto the table of random numbers (Table 31.1), in which any number is as likely to occur as any other. Beginning at the number nearest your pencil point, write down each two-digit number (for example, 03, 08, 15, 62, 79, 98, etc.); continue down one column and up another until you have 20 two-digit numbers. Take the mean of the column (the average). (Your instructor may or may not wish for you to compute the "standard deviation"; instructions are given in Part D.)

Closing your eyes again, find a new starting point and repeat the exercise. Complete at least eight lists of 20 numbers. Compare the means and record them in Table 31.2.

If you repeated the exercise many, many times (preferably using samples larger than $n = 20$) and plotted the means, you would begin to see what is called the *normal curve* (Fig. 31.1). The normal curve represents the tendency for infinite sample means to cluster about the true mean of a population. The normal curve is extremely important in statistical theory and indeed in communications research. If you calculated the standard deviation and the variance of your sample means, you could learn from the curve the extent to which your sample(s) is likely to vary from the true population mean. For instance, it is known that 68% of means in a normal distribution fall within ±1 standard deviation (SD) of the mean; 95% fall within 2 standard deviations (Fig. 31.1). This fact enables you to say (if other requirements of sampling are satisfied), "The mean score that occurred for my sample may not precisely equal the true mean score for the population, but I am X% confident that it is within $\pm X$ standard deviations of the true score." That is the answer to the problem of sample error and sampling distribution: If we can specify the margin by which a score is unlikely to differ from the true mean, we have set important estimates of the accuracy of our results.

The same rationale applies to the interpretation of percentages. That is important because opinion polls (in fact, polls of all types) most often are reported in percentages. Suppose candidate Smith was projected to receive 52% of the vote in next Tuesday's election and Jones was projected to receive 48%. How confident could we be in the accuracy of the projection? The problem lies in sampling error; if we had drawn a sample whose margin of error was 5 percentage points, the winner might turn out to be Jones instead of Smith. From this example, you can see that it is important that a researcher state the sample's margin of error.

Table 31.1. Table of Random Numbers

	00–04	05–09	10–14	15–19	20–24	25–29	30–34	35–39	40–44	45–49
00	54463	22662	65905	70639	79365	67382	29085	69831	47058	08186
01	15389	85205	18850	39226	42249	90669	96325	23248	60933	26927
02	85941	40756	82414	02015	13858	78030	16269	65978	01385	15345
03	61149	69440	11286	88218	58925	03638	52862	62733	33451	77455
04	05219	81619	10651	67079	92511	59888	84502	72095	83463	75577
05	41417	98326	87719	92294	46614	50948	64886	20002	97365	30976
06	28357	94070	20652	35774	16249	75019	21145	05217	47286	76305
07	17783	00015	10806	83091	91530	36466	39981	62481	49177	75779
08	40950	84820	29881	85966	62800	70326	84740	62660	77379	90279
09	82995	64157	66164	41180	10089	41757	78258	96488	88629	37231
10	96754	17676	55659	44105	47361	34833	86679	23930	53249	27083
11	34357	88040	53364	71726	45690	66334	60332	22554	90600	71113
12	06318	37403	49927	57715	50423	67372	63116	48888	21505	80182
13	62111	52820	07243	79931	89292	84767	85693	73947	22278	11551
14	47534	09243	67879	00544	23410	12740	02540	54440	32949	13491
15	98614	75993	84460	62846	59844	14922	48730	73443	48167	34770
16	24856	03648	44898	09351	98795	18644	39765	71058	90368	44104
17	96887	12479	80621	66223	86085	78285	02432	53342	42846	94771
18	90801	21472	42815	77408	37390	76766	52615	32141	30268	18106
19	55165	77312	83666	36028	28420	70219	81369	41943	47366	41067
20	75884	12952	84318	95108	72305	64620	91318	89872	45375	85436
21	16777	37116	58550	42958	21460	43910	01175	87894	81378	10620
22	46230	43877	80207	88877	89380	32992	91380	03164	98656	59337
23	42902	66892	46134	01432	94710	23474	20423	60137	60609	13119
24	81007	00333	39693	28039	10154	95425	39220	19774	31782	49037
25	68089	01122	51111	72373	06902	74373	96199	97017	41273	21546
26	20411	67081	89950	16944	93054	87687	96693	87236	77054	33848
27	58212	13160	06468	15718	82627	76999	05999	58680	96739	63700
28	70577	42866	24969	61210	76046	67699	42054	12696	93758	03283
29	94522	74358	71659	62038	79643	79169	44741	05437	39038	13163
30	42626	86819	85651	88678	17401	03252	99547	32404	17918	62880
31	16051	33763	57194	16752	54450	19031	58580	47629	54132	60631
32	08244	27647	33851	44705	94211	46716	11738	55784	95374	72655
33	59497	04392	09419	89964	51211	04894	72882	17805	21896	83864
34	97155	13428	40293	09985	58434	01412	69124	82171	59058	82859
35	98409	66162	95763	47420	20792	61527	20441	39435	11859	41567
36	45476	84882	65109	96597	25930	66790	65706	61203	53634	22557
37	89300	69700	50741	30329	11658	23166	05400	66669	48708	03887
38	50051	95137	91631	66315	91428	12275	24816	68091	71710	33258
39	31753	85178	31310	89642	98364	02306	24617	09609	83942	22716
40	79152	53829	77250	20190	56535	18760	69942	77448	33278	48805
41	44560	38750	83635	56540	64900	42912	13953	79149	18710	68618
42	68328	83378	63369	71381	39564	05615	42451	64559	97501	65747
43	46939	38689	58625	08342	30459	85863	20781	09284	26333	91777
44	83544	86141	15707	96256	23068	13782	08467	89469	93842	55349
45	91621	00881	04900	54224	46177	55309	17852	27491	89415	23466
46	91896	67126	04151	03795	59077	11848	12630	98375	52068	60142
47	55751	62515	21108	80830	02263	29303	37204	96926	30506	09808
48	85156	87689	95493	88842	00664	55017	55539	17771	69448	87530
49	07521	56898	12236	60277	39102	62315	12239	07105	11844	01117

Source: George W. Snedecor and William G. Cochran, *Statistical Methods*, 7th ed. (Ames: Iowa State University Press, 1980).

Table 31.2. Samples of 20 Numbers Each from Table 31.1

1	2	3	4	5	6	7	8

Means

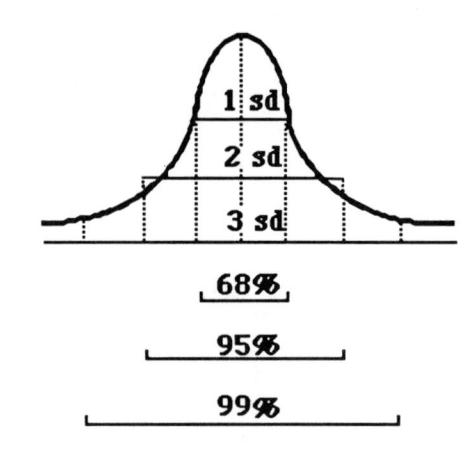

Fig. 31.1. Illustration of the distribution of standard deviation in random sampling.

Part B: Deciding on a sample size. Here is one of the most interesting questions for students of survey research: How can I learn what sample size is required for the survey job that has been requested? Let's begin with the knowledge that as the size of the sample increases (assuming the sample is properly drawn), the amount of error inherent in the sample decreases. No doubt that is comforting news, and it is what you expected. However, the cost of error reduction is great; you must increase the size of your sample four times to reduce the error level by half.

For example, suppose you asked 250 people a yes-no question, and 30% of them said "yes." The margin of error associated with a sample of 250 is about ±5.8 points. Now, if your sample was quadrupled to 1,000, your error margin would be reduced to about 2.9, or half of 5.8. If your sample was 4,000, your error margin would be about 1.4, etc. Seldom are we able to draw samples larger than 1,000 or 2,000, and more usually our samples are 300 to 500. Very small samples (50 to 150) are seldom useful except in special circumstances.

Part C: Calculating sample size.

1. Decide your confidence level (see Unit 29). Let's say that near-perfect confidence is desirable, but you must compromise because of expenses. Let's say you are willing to live with an outcome that should be correct 95 times in 100 samples. We will call that 95% confidence, and we will say that 95% has a confidence "factor" of 1.96, or roughly 2. We will use that factor in the calculations below (99.7% has a confidence factor of about 3).

2. Take the square of the confidence factor: $(1.96)^2 = 3.84$; $(2)^2 = 4$.

3. Decide what error level you can live with. Must your numbers be correct with 1 to 2 points, or could you get by with an error margin of 5 or more? Arbitrarily, we will set our error level at 5.

4. Square the error level: $(5)^2 = 25$.

5. Divide the square of the error level into the square of the confidence factor: 3.84/25 = 0.15.

6. Assume a yes-no type survey situation; if you have no way of estimating the likely percentage for each outcome, take the safe approach and say yes = 50% and no = 50%; i.e., an equal split would yield the greatest uncertainty.

7. Multiply the percentage of yes times the percentage of no: 50 × 50 = 2,500.

8. Multiply the product (0.15) obtained in step 5 times the product obtained in step 7: 2,500 × 0.15 = 375.

Thus if you want to be 95% confident of your outcome within ±5 points, a sample of 384 is required. Note that, in general, this applies to any size population; however, to the extent that you are uncertain of the randomness of the sample, the sample size may have to be increased.

Now perform the above operations with the following numbers and observe how the outcomes vary:

1. Confidence level = 1.96, error level = 2.5, sample size = ?

2. Confidence level = 3, error level = 5, sample size = ?

3. Confidence level = 1.96, error level = 1.75, sample size = ?

4. Confidence level = 3, error level = 2.5, sample size =   ?

Part D. Standard deviation. Here is how to compute standard deviation:

1. List your 20 numbers in a column for addition.
2. Now, take the sum (sum of scores) and square it (example: 50 × 50 = 2,500). Call this the *square of the sum*.
3. Go back and square each number in your column (example: 02 × 02 = 4) and add up the squares. Divide the result by the number of cases (here, 20). Call this the *sum of squares*.
4. Subtract the sum of squares from the square of the sum.
5. Divide that result by $n - 1$ (here, 20 - 1 = 19). Call this the *variance*.
6. Take the square root. This is the standard deviation.

The instructor may ask the class, using a show of hands, to identify the highest and lowest scores without regard to which column of figures they came from. Suppose one student reported an average (for any one column) of 25, and another reported an average for one column of 75. We would subtract the smaller from the larger to obtain the range of scores (that is, all other averages would be between the high and low). We would then divide the range by some number, say 10, to establish increments of difference between scores. If we divide 50 by 10, we would obtain increments of 5. Hence we could devise a chart as shown in Figure 31.2.

The instructor may ask each student to call out his or her averages, rounding each to the nearest whole number. Each time a mean is duplicated, it is simply stacked atop the previous score. Naturally, most scores will occur in the 40 to 60 range; that is the nature of the distribution of means. If luck is with us, our distribution of scores may resemble a normal curve, at least in rough outline.

If we have from 8 to 20 students in class and each calculated 8 means, we would generate 64 to 160. The instructor can plot these means on the board, in the manner of Figure 31.2, to the extent that judgment calls for.

This illustrates that if one draws sufficient means, the distribution will ultimately fall into a predictable pattern, and from this can be determined the likely error of a particular sample of size n.

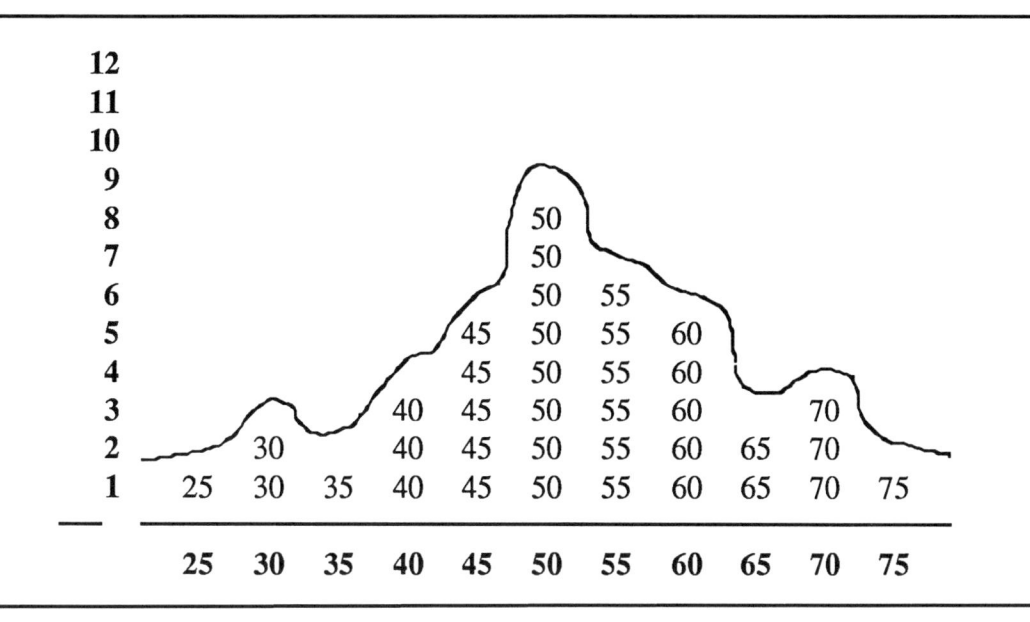

```
12
11
10
 9
 8               50
 7               50
 6               50  55
 5           45  50  55  60
 4           45  50  55  60
 3       40  45  50  55  60      70
 2   30  40  45  50  55  60  65  70
 1 25 30 35 40 45 50 55 60 65 70 75
   ─────────────────────────────────
   25 30 35 40 45 50 55 60 65 70 75
```

Fig. 31.2. Illustrative plot of repeated but not infinite sample means from a population.

GLOSSARY: THE LANGUAGE OF SAMPLING

Sample--A set of "elements" purporting to represent a larger "population." For example, if you cannot query every classmate on whether holiday breaks should be longer, you might ask any selected subset (sample) of the class and hope you could infer their feelings to the rest. Of course, for accuracy, you would have to draw your sample carefully.

Simple random sample--"Simple" only in the sense that it sets a simple requirement: every element in the population must be given an equal opportunity to be included in the sample.

Element--Any unit that is sampled. For example, in your survey of your classmates, the element is the student.

Population--All the elements in a defined setting. For example, at your university, a survey population might be (1) all students enrolled full-time, (2) all male students over age 20, or (3) all freshmen females, etc. The emphasis is on "all," but in a defined way.

Universe--All the elements of the type. For example, a survey sample might be 300 freshmen; a survey population might be all the freshmen on campus; a survey universe might be all the freshmen in the state, nation, or world.

Census--A survey of all the elements in a population or universe.

Sampling unit--Akin to "element." The sampling unit might be individuals, towns, or census blocks, etc.

Sampling frame--The compilation of the sampling unit. For example, the telephone can be a sampling frame as well as the files of the university registrar or the town's list of registered voters.

Parameter--A description of a variable in a population. The parameter is a summary statistic used to describe a population. For example, the average age of university students is a parameter of the population.

Observation unit--Same as "element," the unit from which information is collected.

Sample distribution--The distribution of scores of any single sample. Suppose the height of a tree was 50 feet, and you asked a sample of 200 persons to guess the height. The average guess most likely would not be precisely 50 feet but some number larger or smaller. Let's say the average guess was 46 feet. So if you plotted the 200 guesses, some would be lower (maybe much lower) than 46 feet, and some would be higher (maybe much higher) than 46 feet. The difference between the lowest and highest is the "range." Any sample distribution is likely to deviate from the "true" score, and in this case from the population distribution.

Population distribution--It is conceivable, but unlikely, that you could survey every element of a population and could graph the results, in which case you would see a population distribution. Would the population distribution equal the "true" score? Not necessarily (in the case of the tree height), but the point is that a sample distribution has a known relationship to the population distribution.

Sampling distribution--Suppose your sampling frame was the telephone book, you drew 400 samples of 200 numbers, and then you graphed the means of the 400 samples. Eventually, your graph would take on the appearance of the familiar bell-shaped curve. The point is that the sampling distribution, theoretically, is "normal" (symmetric) even if the population distribution is not. This is a central fact in statistical theory and one that allows many statistical inferences.

Sampling error--Suppose you already knew the average student age on your campus, but as a test of sampling you drew a sample of 400 students and took the average age. Chances are very good that the sample average would not equal the true average. The sample average might be higher or lower, by a lot or a little. The difference between the sample mean and the true mean is called sampling error.

Standard error--Defined as the standard deviation divided by the square root of the sample size. It is analogous to the standard deviation (defined below). Standard error is used in calculating the likely accuracy of a sample mean (which is a population estimate) or a percentage score. As with the standard deviation, about 68% of samples fall within ±1 standard error of the true mean, and 95% fall within ±2 standard errors of the true mean. When standard deviation has not been calculated, standard error can be calculated by taking the square root of percentage P times percentage Q (which is $1 - P$) divided by n.

Margin of error--The range of likely deviation of a sample mean (average) from a population mean, that is, the amount by which a sample mean (if properly obtained) might be expected to deviate from the true mean. Suppose, for example, a population (true) mean was 20.1; for a sample of 600, at the 95% confidence level, the error margin might be (about) ±1.6. That is, you might expect any number between 20.1 plus 1.6 and 20.1 minus 1.6. To see the effect of sample size and percentage response on error margin see Table 31.3.

Confidence level--Addresses the question of how certain we can be about an outcome. Typically, researchers set confidence levels at 95% or 99% (stated as $p = 0.05$ or $p = 0.01$).

Standard deviation--A standardized measure of the extent of variation from the mean.

Table 31.3. Probable Deviation (Plus or Minus) of Results Due to Size of Sample Only (Safety Factor of 20 to 1)

Survey Result Is:	1% or 99%	5% or 95%	10% or 90%	15% or 85%	20% or 80%	25% or 75%	30% or 70%	35% or 65%	40% or 60%	45% or 55%	50%
Sample of: 25	4.0	8.7	12.0	14.3	16.0	17.3	18.3	19.1	19.6	19.8	20.0
50	2.8	6.2	8.5	10.1	11.4	12.3	13.0	13.5	13.9	14.1	14.2
75	2.3	5.0	6.9	8.2	9.2	10.0	10.5	11.0	11.3	11.4	11.5
100	2.0	4.4	6.0	7.1	8.0	8.7	9.2	9.5	9.8	9.9	10.0
150	1.6	3.6	4.9	5.9	6.6	7.1	7.5	7.8	8.0	8.1	8.2
200	1.4	3.1	4.3	5.1	5.7	6.1	6.5	6.8	7.0	7.0	7.1
250	1.2	2.7	3.8	4.5	5.0	5.5	5.8	6.0	6.2	6.2	6.3
300	1.1	2.5	3.5	4.1	4.6	5.0	5.3	5.5	5.7	5.8	5.8
400	.99	2.2	3.0	3.6	4.0	4.3	4.6	4.8	4.9	5.0	5.0
500	.89	2.0	2.7	3.2	3.6	3.9	4.1	4.3	4.4	4.5	4.5
600	.81	1.8	2.5	2.9	3.3	3.6	3.8	3.9	4.0	4.1	4.1
800	.69	1.5	2.1	2.5	2.8	3.0	3.2	3.3	3.4	3.5	3.5
1,000	.63	1.4	1.9	2.3	2.6	2.8	2.9	3.1	3.1	3.2	3.2
2,000	.44	.96	1.3	1.6	1.8	1.9	2.0	2.1	2.2	2.2	2.2
3,000	.36	.79	1.1	1.3	1.5	1.6	1.7	1.7	1.8	1.8	1.8
4,000	.31	.69	.95	1.1	1.3	1.4	1.4	1.5	1.5	1.6	1.6
5,000	.28	.62	.85	1.0	1.1	1.2	1.3	1.4	1.4	1.4	1.4
10,000	.20	.44	.60	.71	.80	.87	.92	.95	.98	.99	1.0
50,000	.08	.17	.24	.29	.32	.35	.37	.38	.39	.40	.40

Source: National Association of Broadcasters, "A Broadcast Research Primer" (Washington, D.C.: NAB, 1976). Used with permission.

Example: When size of sample is 500 and survey result comes out 25%, you may be reasonably sure (odds 20 to 1) that this result is no more than 3.9 off, plus or minus. Doubling the sample to 1,000 reduces this margin to 2.8.

UNIT 32
Questionnaire Design

READING:
Louise H. Kidder. *Research Methods in Social Relations*, 4th ed. New York: Holt, Rinehart, and Winston, 1981, pp. 159-78.

Much theory and research are based on samples of respondents and the responses are only as good as the sample. The same point can be made in regard to questionnaire design. Generating data through questionnaires is easy; generating good data is not.

A guest editorial in the Baltimore *Sun* made the point well. It cited a National Academy of Sciences critique of opinion polling. In an experiment, two questions were asked of different but matched sets of respondents: "Do you think the U.S. should forbid public speeches against democracy?" and "Do you think the U.S. should allow public speeches against democracy?" The editorial said that on the first question 54% of the respondents believed the speeches should be forbidden; but on the second question 75% thought they should not be allowed. Presumably, the connotation of "forbid" is not the same as not allow. The word "forbid" might have been seen as somewhat dictatorial; not allowed might have suggested antecedent conditions.

Thus the writing of questions is fraught with hazards. A single word can matter greatly. A response might be influenced by deference to an interviewer or to an idea, or it might be influenced by the social acceptability of the answer. (For example, suppose it is known that most people read 2 to 3 magazines per month, but you read none; might you exaggerate your reading as a hedge against embarrassment?) The question writer must learn to recognize these problems and to write questions with the greatest care.

EXERCISES

Part A. As an exercise in questionnaire design, let's prepare our own questionnaire. Let's say we want to learn "the extent to which students watch TV." Sounds easy enough, right? You are to write five questions to explore this matter. But follow this rule: don't put anything on paper you wouldn't feel comfortable defending in court! (And you know how "picky" lawyers can be; choose words carefully.)

Consider the words in the research topic. What is meant by "extent"? Does it imply frequency, duration, intensity, or something else? Decide for yourself. What is meant by "students"? Does the word mean college students, grade school students, full-time students, part-time students, upperclassmen, freshmen, etc.? Decide for yourself. What is meant by "watching"? Can the watching be casual, or must it be relatively absorbed? What is meant by relatively? And does the watching have to be recent, or can it be within the past few weeks or months? You see, others don't see our thoughts nearly as clearly as we do!

If we are to study viewing, we must learn whether the respondents have a TV receiver, so we ask, "Do you have a TV?" But the questionnaire writer has to anticipate a range of possible responses. What are some responses that might result from the question, "Do you have a TV?" One might be, "Yes, I have a TV (but it is at home, not here at college)." The parenthetic qualification is important, for it colors the respondent's subsequent answers. Another might say, "Yes, I have a TV (but it is broken and I haven't watched TV in weeks)." Or, "Yes (my *family* owns one)." Or, "Yes (I've had one in the past)." Clearly, different people can use the same words with different interpretations. It is up to the researcher to anticipate this and to account for it.

Before you write your five questions, let's try to improve the statement of the research problem.

<u>Original Statement</u>: We want to learn "the extent to which students watch TV."

Data with which the statement might be improved:

1. Who will be surveyed?
2. How many persons will be surveyed? This is important because it suggests the margin of error.
3. What kind of sample will be used (that is, simple random, stratified, etc.)?
4. What locale or what universe will the sample be drawn from?
5. How will you define nouns and verbs in your statement?
6. Suggest objective measures, for example, percentage based on random sample.

Write your improved statement of the research problem here:

Part B. Now that you have reflected at length on your research problem (that is, what you hope to accomplish), you can begin to write your five survey questions. Devise questions that will reveal viewing habits, not questions that simply ask for demographics (age, sex, occupation, etc.). The questions should move smoothly from one to another. Use care to devise response options that capture a satisfactory range of possibilities.

Question 1.

Critique:

Question 2.

Critique:

Question 3.

Critique:

Question 4.

Critique:

Question 5.

Critique:

UNIT 33 *Readability*

READING:
Rudolf Flesch. "A New Readability Yardstick." *Journal of Applied Psychology* 32(1948):221-33.

Ron Smith. "How Consistently Do Readability Tests Measure the Difficulty of Newswriting." *Newspaper Research Journal* 5(1984): 1-8.

For communication to take place, a message must be encoded, transmitted, received, and decoded (comprehended). Comprehension can be a matter of degree; one can comprehend a lot, a little, or not much at all. Presumably, most professional communicators have substantial success, yet there are times when the degree of success is uncertain. Failure to communicate adequately can be caused by channel factors (for example, radio static or telephone line noise), source factors (a source might lack credibility), receiver factors (a receiver might be easily distracted or inept), or encoding factors (for example, the choice of inappropriate symbols or those not shared by the receiver).

EXERCISES

Part A. This exercise emphasizes encoding and comprehension. To what degree does the communicator succeed in transferring meaning from point A (the sender) to point B (the receiver)? Encoding is the major task of the media communicator; it requires conversion of complex events into symbols carrying denotative and connotative information. (For elaboration of the latter terms, see Unit 36.) In plain terms, we are referring here to the study of readability, whether "the stuff that you write is the same stuff that I understand."

Readability is important in both practical terms (the marketplace) and theoretical terms (growth of knowledge). For purposes of theory, we can examine communication for evidence of systems and patterns; we can look for language cadence, structure, or unstated meanings. Such knowledge helps in the prediction of successful communication, at least up to a point. For purposes of the marketplace, theory aside, we can examine readability as a way of assuring that our audiences are being served. For example, suppose you are an editor with great, even exaggerated, respect for language; you love the neat word, the well-turned phrase, elaborate prose with delicate subtleties. Suppose over the years your writing, and presumably that of the staff you influence, improved, but the skills of your audience, on average, did not change. You risk leaving your audience behind, not a desirable outcome for the communicator!

Media communicators, especially media managers, need to know the basics of readability measurement. They need to be able to assess whether they are communicating *to* their audience, *above* them, or *below* them. As you will see in the following paragraphs, measurement as it is known today is imprecise, but at the very least it provides a rough yardstick, a measure that, if followed with intuition and judgment, can be useful.

Studies of readability are some of the old-timers, so to speak, of the relatively young field of communications research. That is, readability has not been an active area of research for perhaps 20 years or more. For our purpose, we will suggest that the studies date from the 1920s to the 1950s. They were aimed at development of formulas that could estimate whether communication was satisfactory. Over the years, many have been proposed. Unfortunately, different formulas sometimes produced different solutions, depending on the language conditions of the passage under study.

But put yourself in the place of the researcher. If you were studying readability, what would you look for? First, you would have to ask, What is meant by readability? Presumably, it means comprehension, not reading speed. Curiously, most of the formulas do not measure comprehension; they measure characteristics of the language. If you were studying characteristics of the language, what would you look for? Think about how one word is different from another. Below, list several distinctions one might make.

Some differences between words:

(Example: number of letters per word)

Some differences between sentences:

(Example: number of words per sentence)

Part B. Now that you have attempted to identify some of the characteristics of words and sentences, let's review some of the approaches used by researchers. It might be a little humbling to learn that there may be dozens of language or organizational elements that can have a bearing on readability!

One early study (1920s) was based largely on the idea of word frequency. If a word occurred frequently, then it should be familiar and understanding should be enhanced. In what must have been tedious work indeed, 10,000 of the most common words were ranked for frequency; the most frequent words were given high numbers (into 3 digits) and the low-frequency words, low numbers. Rare words (those not on the 10,000-word list) were numbered zero. The technique was to select samples of 1,000 words, then to compute vocabulary range (total number of different words per thousand), zero-value words (rare words) per thousand, and the median word-value score. But the resulting score had no particular meaning of its own; it required a comparison with another sample. One might distinguish between, say, two books, but not get a lot of meaning from one score alone.

Skipping forward into the 1940s, we turn to the work of Rudolf Flesch; his work became something of an industry standard, although certainly not the only applied formula. Flesch first tried to use the concept of word abstractness; he developed his own list of nearly 14,000 words. But subsequently he found that the number of affixes (prefixes and suffixes) was about as good an estimator as abstractness. Then he found that some 3- to 4-letter words could be more difficult than some longer words, and he finally discarded abstractness altogether.

Flesch concluded readability could be measured in terms of what he called reading ease and human interest. He developed formulas for each. Reading ease was calculated by the following method.[1] Multiply the average sentence length (sample of 100 sentences) by 1.015; multiply the number of syllables per 100 words by .846; add the two products; then subtract 206.835. The resulting score would be between 0 and 100. Flesch said a score near 0 would be virtually unreadable, while a score of 90 to 100 would be very easy "for any literate person." A score of 80 to 90 would be appropriate for a sixth grade reading level, while a score of 50 to 60 was considered "fairly difficult," suitable for tenth through twelfth grade reading skills. A score of 30 to 50 was considered college level reading, and a score of 0 to 30 was "very difficult."

---

1. Rudolf Flesch, *The Art of Readable Writing* (New York: Harper and Row, 1949), pp. 213-16.

But Flesch argued that readability consisted of not only reading ease but also human interest. For instance, a person might be more attracted to material that was relevant on a personal level. Flesch defined human interest as the use of personal words and personal references. Personal words referred to people or named people. Words referring to people included personal pronouns but not neutral pronouns. He calculated human interest in the following way. Multiply the number of personal words per 100 words by 3.635; multiply the number of personal sentences per 100 sentences by .314; add the products. The result is the human interest score, falling somewhere between 0 and 100. Zero suggests "no human interest," while 100 suggests the material is "full of human interest." In general, the lower the score, the less interesting the material. Any score between 0 and 10 identified the writing as "dull." A score of 10 to 20 indicated "mildly interesting," while 20 to 40 was "interesting." A score of 40 to 60 was "highly interesting," and 60 to 100 was "dramatic."

Flesch's formulas were published in the 1940s. Would you expect them to be accurate predictors of reading skill today? Why? (Is a tenth grade reading skill today the same as in 1949?) Write your answer below.

In the early 1950s, Robert Gunning offered a slightly simpler estimate of readability. His system was based on average sentence length in words and number of words of three syllables or more per 100 words. The two scores should be added and multiplied by 0.4. The resulting score estimates the school grade level for which the material is written.

Wayne Danielson and Sam Bryan developed a computer program in 1963 that took the labor out of counting and computing scores and provided a readability score similar to the Flesch score.

Finally, we should examine the cloze procedure developed by Wilson L. Taylor in 1955. This approach is based on one aspect of information theory, namely, redundancy. Most of us, it seems, routinely rely on a very small portion of the many thousands of words available to us; we rely on 1,500 to 2,000 for casual conversation. Using so few different words, one can readily imagine that many words occur again and again. The principle of the cloze procedure is that if the words occur with frequency, they can be predicted with accuracy; the greater the accuracy, the simpler or clearer the message.

Consider this sentence: "_____ first time I saw Paris, we _____ traveling with a group from Germany." If you stop and think for a moment, you probably can guess the missing words. The first word should be "the," and the second should be "were." Suppose each nth word was missing from a longer passage; the extent to which you could accurately supply the missing word would indicate the difficulty of the passage. That is the principle of the cloze procedure (named after the tendency to seek closure in meanings).

Let's try our hand at filling the blanks of a cloze passage. Refer to the following sentences. There are 24 blanks. The list of missing words is at the end of the exercise, but *do not refer to the list at this time*. First, go to the passage and fill in the blanks as best you can. When you have done that, refer to the list of words at the end of the exercise. Count your number of incorrect guesses and subtract from 24. Divide the remainder by 24 to produce your percentage of correct responses. Example: Suppose you guessed 16 words correctly; divide 24 into 16. Your percentage will be 66. The instructor may wish to find the range of scores for the class and thus to estimate the average difficulty of the passage.

Given the wide variety of _____ to research, it stands to _____ that the possible approaches to _____ a research report are equally _____. However, some comfort may be _____ from the fact that most _____ reports include five basic sections _____ chapters: (1) an introduction, (2) a review of _____ and/or a justification, (3) a description _____ methodologies, (4) a presentation of results, _____ (5) a summary or conclusion. This _____ is used both in articles _____ professional publication and in management _____.

The purpose of this section _____ to describe some of the _____ for writing research reports. Beginning researchers _____ find the writing style awkward _____ un-aesthetic, but there is _____ definite purpose behind the rules _____ scientific writing: clarity. Every effort

164

_____ be made to avoid ambiguity. _____ journals' and businesses' writing requirements _____ vary in some details, the _____ suggestions are applicable to _____ types of reports. (See list of missing words at the end of this unit.)[1]

Research indicates that, generally, a score over 61% shows "independent level" reading (not excessively difficult), whereas a score of 41% shows the material to be rather difficult. The numbers make sense; if you guessed every word correctly, your score would be 100% and the material clearly would have been easy. If you guessed 50%, you would be between "extremely easy" and "impossible"; if you guessed only 25% of the correct words and your score was comparable to others, the material clearly would have been difficult.

<u>Part C</u>. How does the cloze procedure stack up against the other measures of readability? In one way, it may be better. It accounts for the possibility that a very short word may be a very difficult word to comprehend. But let's compare for ourselves. Let's evaluate the passage with both the Flesch and Gunning formulas.

Enter your calculations here:

<u>Reading ease (Flesch)</u>: 206.835 − .846 × average syllables per 100 words − 1.015 × average words per sentence. (Refer to the formula discussed in Part B.)

    a. .846 × average syllables per 100 words = _____

    b. 1.015 × average words per sentence = _____

    c. Add (a) and (b) = _____

    d. Subtract the sum of (a) and (b) from 206.835 = _____

    e. Reading ease = _____

For interpretation, see discussion in Part B.

<u>Gunning's fog index</u>: (based on sample of 100 words)

    a. Count 100 words and divide by the number of sentences.

    b. Enter average sentence length here: _____

    c. Count the number of words of three syllables or more: _____

---

1. Cloze passage taken from Roger D. Wimmer and Joseph R. Dominick, *Mass Media Research* (Belmont, Calif.: Wadsworth, 1983), p. 347.

d. Add (b) and (c): _____

e. Multiply the final score in (d) by 0.4: _____

f. Enter grade level difficulty: _____

Review the three scores (Flesch and Gunning above and Taylor's cloze procedure) and answer the following questions:

1. Are the scores consistent?

2. Is there any dispute about definitions? Is the procedure absolutely objective?

3. Does either approach to readability fail to take into account important aspects of language?

4. Does it seem reasonable to you that two characteristics of a paragraph could accurately estimate the difficulty of the passage for comprehension?

5. To what degree is error involved in the computation? That is, if the formulas are not entirely accurate, how well do they work?

Missing words, Taylor's cloze procedure:

approaches
reason
writing
varied
derived
research
or
literature
of
and
format
for

summaries
is
basics
may
or
a
governing
must
Although
may
following
most

UNIT 34
Content Analysis

READING:
Morris Janowitz. "Content Analysis and the Study of Sociopolitical Change." *Journal of Communication* 26(1976):10-21.

Content analysis is a popular research method in mass communications because access to media content is readily at hand. Since the message is disseminated widely, researchers can gain access to copies of the print media and to audio- and videotapes of the broadcast media. It is possible then to analyze the messages of mass media after they have been published, in as much detail as necessary for a variety of purposes. For instance, we can compare the content of competing publications in the same medium--cartoons on ABC vs. those on NBC, articles in *Newsweek* vs. those in *Time*, a morning paper in a city with an afternoon paper there.

But with content analysis we can make other kinds of comparisons and analyses. By closely analyzing the content of a known liberal or conservative publication, we might be able to determine what the writers or editors intended their readers to gain from a particular message or set of messages. Hence we can make inferences about the intent the message providers might have.

Depending on our method of content analysis, we can observe differences in message style, readability, length, placement, visuals, etc. A host of investigative applications is available.

There are a number of steps necessary to be able to perform a content analysis with both reliability and validity. Remember that *reliability* means that a researcher following another's methods exactly would be likely to obtain the same results. *Validity* means one's methods of research have been properly designed to measure what was intended to be measured. It would not be valid to try to determine the education level of a given magazine's adult audience by analyzing the size of the type in headlines. That might give us a measure of the audience's age (the smaller the type, the younger the audience, since eyesight gets worse with age, generally speaking). But to infer education level, we would have to analyze the difficulty of the text: How many words per 100 words have three or more syllables? How long are the sentences? It would be valid to assume that the more difficult the text is to read and understand, the more educated readers are likely to be (see Unit 33).

Kerlinger's definition of content analysis embodies all the necessary characteristics.[1] He said it was the systematic, objective, and quantitative manner of studying communication messages to measure variables. We know then that we are dealing with a numerical scheme that has to be administered in a prescribed manner, consistently, and in a way that eliminates opinion. Here are the steps with some explanation of what they demand:

1. Form research questions or hypotheses. To determine what has been discovered at the end of a content analysis project, it is necessary to begin with the statements of relationships we think exist. We might hypothesize that *Time* magazine provides more coverage of Middle Eastern countries than European countries.

2. Define the population. Are we including all issues of *Time* from the 1930s through today or just issues during the past three years? Let's say we include only the past three years.

3. Select a sample from the population. Since there might be 1,000 articles on coverage of nations we are interested in during the three-year period, we can reduce the amount of work we need to do by selecting, in a random manner, one issue per month during the 36 months. (See Unit 31, Part A.)

4. Define a unit of analysis. Will we define a story on one of these countries as any story with a headline, as a story with a picture, or limit the unit of analysis to only one story per page? We will decide to include every story with a headline.

5. Construct categories of content to be analyzed. We can deal with only two here: (a) locality, for which we would take the dateline of the article, that is, Egypt, England, etc., and (b) length, or how long the story is in column inches.

6. Determine a system of quantification. One measure would be to count a story in either the European category or the Middle Eastern category as one entry per story related to a headline on that topic. Another would be to count column inches with a ruler, but here we would have a measurement problem because not all stories will be placed across the page in three-column layout. Some may have two 1½-column lengths across the page. This difficulty would have to be worked out in square inches or in just counting the number of stories rather than the column inches, but the critical need is that each coder who may be measuring column inches measure them in the same prescribed manner.

7. Do a pilot study to determine reliability. Here it is necessary to go through the coding process once with all coders to see if their decisions agree. We would like a 90% agreement level or above. If we don't, we need to more carefully define the coding scheme for the categories. (See Unit 35.)

---

1. F. Kerlinger, *Foundations of Behavioral Research*, 2d ed. (New York: Holt, Rinehart, and Winston, 1973).

8. Code content. Let the coders do their thing. The researcher shouldn't participate and the coders should not be aware of the exact purpose of the study.

9. Analyze the data collected. Use charts or computer analysis.

10. Draw conclusions from the data. Decide whether the data support the hypothesis.

EXERCISE

With the above background, let's actually do a content analysis project based on one reported in *Journalism Quarterly*.[2]

Here the objective is to determine the extent of bad news over good news on television. For your exercise, let's make it your local NBC television network affiliate, or that of a nearby metropolitan area if you don't have a local station. You might want to choose another affiliate, and that is all right too, as long as everyone is using the same one. Your hypothesis is that bad news predominates on the station's local newscast in the early evening (the 5:30 P.M. or 6 P.M. news show).

The population for the study is this selected station's early evening newscast. We will make it the first half-hour if it is a longer show. Instead of selecting a sample, let's just do one show (or two if there is a big class) and handle it as if we were doing the pretest for this project.

The unit of analysis will be the story. You make the decisions on which parts of the newscast will be examined. (Stories can be found on each of the following, but you may not wish to include all.)

1. News: ____yes ____no
2. Weather: ____yes ____no
3. Sports: ____yes ____no
5. Business, stocks: ____yes ____no

When you have decided which stories will be included or excluded from your content analysis, look at Table 34.1. It is a coding sheet and contains all the information you need to construct categories of content to be analyzed (step 5 of the content analysis process).

For this topic, step 5 is the most difficult to deal with because we have to come up with definitions of what constitutes bad news vs. good news. It is a complex problem, which has appeared frequently in the research literature, but no one has established definitions that have been accepted as the model to go by. How will you decide on a

---

2. Gerald C. Stone and Elinor Grusin, "Network TV as the Bad News Bearer," *Journalism Quarterly* 61 (autumn 1984), pp. 517-23, 592.

definition that will allow your coders to place a given story in the right category (good or bad) at a 90% reliability rate?

If you stop here for discussion, you will note immediately that you would need a set of instructions as thick as a zip code book for coders to use in making their decisions. But there won't be time as a 15-second story whizzes by. There is the difficulty of individual decisions. A conservative coder may consider a liberal politician's election bad news, etc. Then there is the problem of quantity. If a story is 60% good news and 40% bad news, which category does it go in? Also, there are close decisions: Student rally at local chemical plant results in temporary shutdown; a prisoner on death row is stabbed, etc. In all, you are dealing with a broad category that seems to defy coding. Can you solve this problem?

Here is the way the article authors solved it. They defined good news as anything the majority of people in this locality (your city) would consider good news. Examples were a building being built or a business opening. Good news was upbeat and positive. Bad news was exactly the opposite: a building being torn down or a business closing, downbeat or negative news. Using these very broad categories, your coders will reach the same decision on about three-quarters of the stories in a newscast. Unfortunately, that is not enough.

The solution was to use the third category: indeterminate news. This was a category coders could use if they simply couldn't decide if the story was good or bad, if they thought the story was equally balanced between good and bad, or if they thought most people in the community wouldn't consider the story either good news or bad. Coders were urged to use the indeterminable category only as a last resort, that is, only if they had strained to make a decision between good and bad but simply could not.

Finally, all coder disagreements in the news value category were thrown into the indeterminate category. Hence if one coder said a story was good news and the other said it was anything else, that story went into the indeterminate category. If you do this project as a class, you probably won't be able to do that, since there will be very few stories on a newscast for which a dozen or more coders will reach agreement. But the exercise is still interesting because you can count the errors in this category and see how that might affect the overall reliability rating.

Other categories to be included are the story number (which will be used later to determine how early in the news show a certain story appeared; the place of story origination, if it's local, state, regional, or national; story length; and whether the story had a film or video clip that ran with part of it (some moving visual as opposed to a "talking head" or still graphic).

Step 6 is the system of quantification. Note here that there are two measures that seem very precise (the origination point and the story length) but that really will constitute only a best guess, since we aren't going to provide coders either a map or a stopwatch. Yet we shouldn't anticipate much disagreement in either category. If we do, we could change the quantification system; for instance, coders would probably have less trouble agreeing on whether the story was in the city area, in the state, or anywhere out of state (the regional classification may cause problems). Actually, Stone and Grusin had the most trouble with the time category because many television news stories are produced in segments lasting either 15 or 30 seconds. If a story is very close to 30 seconds in length, coders are almost equally likely to call it 15 to 29 as they are to call it 30 to 60. Story length, the seemingly most precise category (it can be measured with a stopwatch), was even less precise than determining good versus bad news. In any event the story origination point has a 1 to 4 code; length has a 1 to 4 category code; the news value item will be quantified if the coder merely puts a check in one of the three columns (good news, bad news, indeterminate); and the film clips category can be checked if there is a film clip. Later, when the sheets are completed, we can apply numbers to the news value triad and to the film clips category.

    The next step is to do a half-hour of coding by the form and then go through an intercoder reliability check, as discussed in Unit 35.

Table 34.1. TV Good News vs. Bad News Coding Sheet

Channel:____ Network:____ Date:_____ News Time:_____

Story No.	Short Slug For Story	Origination[a]	Story Length[b]	Good News	Bad News	Indeterminate	Included Film Clip
1							
2							
3							
4							
5							
6							
7							
8							
9							
10							
11							
12							
13							
14							
15							
16							
17							
18							
19							
20							

[a] Story origination code: (1) local, (2) in state but out of city area, (3) regional, but out of state, (4) national, but out of region.

[b] Story length code: (1) under 15 seconds, (2) 15 to 29 seconds, (3) 30 to 60 seconds, (4) over 60 seconds.

Coder name:_____

UNIT 35
Reliability of Measurements in Content Analysis

READING:
William A. Scott. "Reliability of Content Analysis: The Case of Nominal Scale Coding." *Public Opinion Quarterly* 19(fall 1955): 321-25.

Suppose a friend told you the following: "I'm tired of seeing bad news in the newspaper every day. Why, I looked through the last two issues of the paper, and I'd say 40% of the stories involved violence and disaster." In a sense, your friend was conducting research, albeit primitive and probably imprecise. The friend was using *content analysis*, a social science research technique to generate data with which to address a question or problem.

How certain can you be of the accuracy of your friend's assessment? Let's look at several trouble spots:

1. Your friend spoke of "the" newspaper, so the study involved a sample of one. The newspaper may or may not be like any other newspaper; we don't know, so we can't generalize.
2. Which issue of the paper did your friend examine, and why? Was the examination spurred by an uncommon (unrepresentative) spate of stories of violence? Why only two issues? Wouldn't accuracy be improved by increasing the size of the sample?
3. By looking at consecutive issues, did your friend mistakenly think that news carried over from the first day was different news?
4. What was your friend's definition of bad news? That is important, for it sets the percentage score for the study. If two people use different definitions, they are likely to get different results.
5. Did your friend examine just the front page, or were the inside pages included? What was the definition of story? Is the Ann Landers column a story? Again, this could have a great bearing on the final percentage a study tallies.

Each of these criticisms points to the need for what is referred to in research as "reliability." The term poses the following question: If two persons, using the same criteria, examine the same material (here, newspaper content), would they reach the same conclusions about the nature of the material? In interpretation of data that lead to theory, reliability is essential.

Suppose you were to follow behind your friend to check his or her study. You pick two different issues of the newspaper, or even the same two issues. The results you would obtain would either be like

174

those of your friend or different; in either case, there are points that need to be raised. If the data are markedly different, it is fairly easy to disregard them as unreliable. Proper procedure would be to identify likely sources of error and to repeat the study with greater rigor. But suppose the two sets of data are markedly similar. Suppose your friend categorized each story and found 40% involved bad news, whereas you found 38%. Would you feel safe that your friend's study was fairly accurate?

Perhaps, but it would depend on certain things. Suppose the numbers were similar, but you called A, B, and C bad news, while your friend called D, E, and F bad news. You got similar results, but with different data. Instead let's say you called A, B, and C bad news and your friend called A, B, and D bad news. You could say the two coders were 66% accurate (they agreed on 2 of 3). But another possibility is that one or two of the "correct" responses were accidental. In any forced choice situation, a certain amount of agreement can be expected. If you give me three choices and ask me to make a proper selection, I will be "right" one-third of the time just by chance. The point is, even percentage reliability scores can be misleading.

Let's say one researcher examined 100 news stories and found that 40 of them contained bad news. A second researcher examined the same set of stories and agreed with the first on 35 of the 40 stories. Five errors would represent an error rate of 5/40, or 12.5%, or an accuracy rate of 87.5%. Such an accuracy rate sounds satisfactory, since content analysis research is seldom 100% reliable. But if some of our correct answers were due to blind luck, we need to adjust the percentage score. There are several possibilities, but we wish to focus on one, Scott's pi.

William A. Scott, then of the Institute for Social Research at the University of Michigan, published a brief article on reliability in *Public Opinion Quarterly* in the fall of 1955. The article is widely cited, and it is one of several approaches designed to improve estimates of reliability.

Scott's formula for pi is

$$Pi = \frac{(Po - Pe)}{(1 - Pe)}$$

where Po = percentage observed agreement, and Pe = percentage agreement expected on basis of chance.

The only stumbling block in the formula is in the calculation of the percentage agreement expected on the basis of chance. Merely square and sum the percentage of responses found in each response option. For instance, if one coder classified 60% of the stories as neutral news, 15% good news, and 25% bad news, you would square and add $(60\%)^2 + (15\%)^2 + (25\%)^2 = 0.44 = Pe$. The second step in the formula would be to establish the percentage agreement between two coders. For convenience, let's say two coders agreed 80% of the time. Now let's put the two figures, 0.44 and 0.80, into the formula:

$$\frac{(0.80 - 0.44)}{(1 - 0.44)} = \frac{0.36}{0.56} = 0.64 = pi$$

The pi score tells us that the adjusted reliability of the coding scheme (adjusted to account for chance agreements) was considerably more modest than the simple 80% agreement we first observed. We are thus warned to interpret our results with greatest caution, or to throw out the data and try an improved coding scheme.

EXERCISE

What follows is an exercise in which you are encouraged to use Scott's pi. First, select a newspaper. It is likely to be the daily that serves your city. Examine the stories in the paper and decide whether they are good news, bad news, or neutral or indeterminate (undecided). When you have evaluated 20 stories, beginning on page one, you should ask another member of your class to evaluate the same stories. (You should keep your copies of the paper and pass those to your partner.)

Use Table 35.1 to record your evaluations, but don't let your partner see your evaluations. This will test the extent to which you and your partner agree on the categorization of stories. Then make a correction for the possibility that your agreements are a function of chance. This is not a test of your skill or knowledge, and the exercise should pose no threat in any way. It is merely to test the coding reliability.

Here are some special instructions. No doubt stories will include some good news and some bad news; you will have to decide the overall tenor of a story. If it is mostly one type or another, classify it by its dominant emphasis. Don't code weather information unless it is in the news form; don't code photos, cutlines, or teasers (unless teasers have sufficient information to be considered stories). Don't rate headlines separate from stories. Don't skip over any bona fide story.

Scott's pi applies to pairs of coders, but often the coding involves more than two. In such a case, the student should consider using (1) an approach proposed by J. L. Fless, "Measuring Nominal Scale Agreement Among Many Raters," *Psychological Bulletin* 76(1971): 378-82, or (2) an approach suggested by Robert Craig, "Generalization of Scott's Index of Intercoder Agreement," *Public Opinion Quarterly* 45(1981):260-64. If the student's concern is the homogeneity of responses to a set of items, the test of reliability might be the Kuder-Richardson coefficient. See James Bruning and B. L. Kintz, *Computational Handbook of Statistics*, 2d ed. (Glenview, Ill.: Scott, Foresman, 1977).

Table 35.1. Coding Form for the Reliability Exercise

Story (headline)	Newspaper	Page	Good News	Bad News	Neutral News
1.					
2.					
3.					
4.					
5.					
6.					
7.					
8.					
9.					
10.					
11.					
12.					
13.					
14.					
15.					
16.					
17.					
18.					
19.					
20.					

Name: _____

Data Summary and Reliability Analysis

1. Total number of stories examined:_____

2. Percentage of stories classified as "neutral" news:_____ (Avoid "undecided.")

3. Percentage of stories classified as "good" news:_____

4. Percentage of stories classified as "bad" news:_____

For items 2, 3, and 4 above, square the percentage and enter here:

Neutral news:____   Add the three squares:____

Good news:____   The sum is Pe = % expected

Bad news:____

To establish the Po in the Scott formula, it will be necessary for you to work with another student. That other person should examine the same set of stories you worked with and indicate in his or her own workbook whether the story was good, bad, or neutral. Compare the two sets of codes. For each agreement, enter a +; for each disagreement enter a -. Count the number of agreements and divide by the total number of stories. The result will be the percentage agreement between the two coders. For example, if you examined 20 stories and agreed on 16, you would be 80% in agreement. Now you will be set to work the formula. Merely substitute the numbers you generated into the symbols of the formula and carry out the requested functions.

Indicate pi here:_____

If possible, discuss in class how your pi compares with calculations by others in the class.

UNIT 36
Semantic Differential

READING:
Charles E. Osgood, Edward E. Ware, and Charles Morris. "Analysis of the Connotative Meanings of a Variety of Human Values as Expressed by American College Students." *Journal of Abnormal and Social Psychology* 62(1961):62-73.

The *semantic differential* was devised in the context of "the measurement of meaning" by Osgood, Tannenbaum, and Suci at the University of Illinois in the early 1950s.[1] Today, the semantic differential is one of the most used, and perhaps abused, measuring instruments in social science research. Variations are applied to all manner of research designs. One can observe that, at its best, the semantic differential is a fine tool. At its worst (due to poor research techniques, not inherent weakness of the instrument) it can lead to wrong conclusions. This unit is designed to familiarize the student with the technique and its uses.

David Berlo had made the point that "meanings" are not found in words; they are found in us. In other words, a word such as "desk" does not have one standard meaning shared by all; the meaning of the word depends on the intent and the frame of reference of the user. For instance, there are wooden desks, metal desks, Formica-topped desks, desks with "character," old desks, city desks, news desks, etc. The meaning of the word desk depends on the person who uses it and the extent to which the intent of the user is transferred to the listener.

Osgood conceptualized *semantic space;* a word was said to occupy three-dimensional space, and the meaning of a word could be traced in any direction from utter meaninglessness to infinite meaning. And rather than a single meaning, a word might have a "cluster" of meanings. These meanings, which transcend dictionary definitions ("denotative" meaning), are the stuff of what is called "connotative" meanings. Thus many of the feelings a person has about a word or object can be represented as clusters in semantic space.

The clusters are determined through statistical analysis known as *factor analysis.* Osgood and his colleagues found that meanings typically involved three types of clusters; evaluation, potency, and activity.

---

1. Charles E. Osgood, George J. Suci, and Percy H. Tannenbaum, *The Measurement of Meaning* (Urbana, Ill.: University of Illinois Press, 1971), pp. 82-84.

Evaluation is the affective or positive-negative aspect of the word/concept. Potency refers to characteristics of strength. Activity refers to fluidity or dynamism.

The evaluative aspect of meaning has become extremely important in the measurement of attitudes. For example, a series of evaluative words might be grouped and used as an index (a summative measure) of attitude, provided there is evidence of the indexability of the words. Inappropriate indexing is a special problem that can spring from unwise use of the semantic differential. Let us hypothesize, for example, that "attitude" equals the sum of seven selected semantic scales. The attitude, or the attitude object, would be the concept rated by the seven scales (defined in the exercise at the end of the unit), as follows:

Attitude Object: Police Officer

good ___ ___ ___ ___ ___ ___ ___ bad
      7   6   5   4   3   2   1

kind ___ ___ ___ ___ ___ ___ ___ cruel
      7   6   5   4   3   2   1

etc.

The center point on the semantic-differential scale is "undecided" or "no opinion," but the two are not necessarily the same. "No opinion" can mean the respondent has no feeling at all for the object, whereas "undecided" can imply feeling but indecision. The undecided/no opinion option is included because we do not wish to force respondents into a positive/negative choice when in fact they might have no choice or may be undecided. Finally, it can be noted that the seven response options can be scored either +3 to -3, or from 1 to 7. For most purposes, the latter is satisfactory. The researcher must decide whether to make the positive or the negative the low number, then apply it consistently.

The respondent would rate "police officer" on each of the scales. But suppose one or more of the scales was found to measure different dimensions. Perhaps one set of scales measured one dimension (whatever it might be) and another scale or set of scales measured different dimensions. The dimensions might even be offsetting, one slightly positive and one slightly negative. In such a case, if you attempt to combine (index) the scales, your results might be highly misleading. This problem is addressed by using factor analysis to assure that scales measure the same dimensions. Let's say that you used a set of 10 scales; factor analysis might show that 7 of them are mathematically related, that is, they cluster on one dimension or underlying factor. But perhaps 2 of the scales form a second small cluster, and the final scale suggests yet another dimension. Armed with this evidence, we would throw out the 3 unneeded scales but keep the 7 remaining and use them as an index (summative score) of attitude toward police officer.

You have seen above that the semantic differential scales use what are called polar (opposite) adjectives, for example, good-bad, cruel-kind, weak-strong, etc. The scales typically offer seven response options. Care must be taken to ensure that response options are approximately equidistant and that opposite adjectives actually are opposite. For example, is "untrained" the opposite of "skilled"? Would we be wiser to use skilled vs. unskilled? Is "primitive" an opposite for "civilized"? Similar care must be used in naming response options. For example, if we descended from extremely to somewhat to slightly, would the three distinctions be equidistant? Guidance in naming response options for the semantic differential is given in the exercise at the end of this unit. Most instruments do not offer more than seven options on each positive-negative continuum because semantic gradations become blurred.

Following is a sample set of semantic scales. First read carefully the section giving instructions for completing the semantic differential. Apply each of the adjective scales to the concept "police officer." Do not skip any scale; mark only one space per scale.

Attitude Object: Police Officer

sharp	_____ _____ _____ _____ _____ _____ _____	dull
good	_____ _____ _____ _____ _____ _____ _____	bad
strong	_____ _____ _____ _____ _____ _____ _____	weak
efficient	_____ _____ _____ _____ _____ _____ _____	inefficient
desirable	_____ _____ _____ _____ _____ _____ _____	undesirable
kind	_____ _____ _____ _____ _____ _____ _____	cruel
knowledgeable	_____ _____ _____ _____ _____ _____ _____	ignorant
active	_____ _____ _____ _____ _____ _____ _____	passive
soft	_____ _____ _____ _____ _____ _____ _____	hard
helping	_____ _____ _____ _____ _____ _____ _____	hurting
satisfactory	_____ _____ _____ _____ _____ _____ _____	unsatisfactory
necessary	_____ _____ _____ _____ _____ _____ _____	unnecessary
mobile	_____ _____ _____ _____ _____ _____ _____	immobile
quick	_____ _____ _____ _____ _____ _____ _____	slow
happy	_____ _____ _____ _____ _____ _____ _____	sad
competent	_____ _____ _____ _____ _____ _____ _____	incompetent

You may notice that the positive form of each adjective pair is consistently on one side of the instrument above. It is often desirable to alternate the response options from side to side, to avoid "response bias," the tendency of individuals to become mechanical (thoughtless) in completing the rating. The flip side of the problem is that reversed scales may cause some respondents to make errors. But let's assume that you have made no errors, and that we can go forward with our analysis of the marks.

Semantic differential scales are not designed for analysis of a single respondent, so the instructor may wish to examine the responses in class to tally them for several persons. Ideally, although it will not be possible in many cases, the instructor might run the data in a factor analysis to identify scales that cluster, that is, have a mathematical relationship and identify an underlying dimension. On the basis of the factor analysis, an index of scales might be formed on which responses could be examined.

If factor analysis is not feasible, a simpler approach is available. The class could be separated into two groups, male and female, to see if attitude toward "police officer" is different as a function of sex. For scoring, let's call the most positive response 7, the next most positive 6, etc., and the least positive (the worst) 1. Each student should sum his or her own scores. The instructor can sum the scores for the men and women and make a casual comparison of the averages. The t-test or analysis of variance (ANOVA) might be used to test the difference.

Tally Form: Semantic Differential

    1. For each adjective pair (for example, sharp-dull), give yourself a score from 7 to 1.
    2. Total the scores of the 16 adjective pairs.
    3. At the blackboard, or using a calculator, the instructor should total the scores of all students of each sex in the class.
    4. Divide the total for each sex by the number in each group.

    Your average_____

    Group average, male: _____

    Group average, female: _____

If the t-test or ANOVA is used, table data as follows:

Female Scores	Male Scores
1. (average score)	1. (average score)
2.	2.
3.	3.

etc., for the number of students in the class.

EXERCISE

Instructions for Completing the Semantic Differential

In *The Measurement of Meaning*, Osgood et al. offer typical instructions for completing the semantic differential. First, the researcher should identify a concept to measure; second, the researcher should generate a set of semantic scales (for example, good-bad, fair-unfair); third, the respondent should check one of seven blanks per scale. The respondent is to decide to what extent the scale item is related to the research concept. For example, if the scale is very closely related to the concept, the respondent would check as follows:

fair X ___ ___ ___ ___ ___ ___ unfair

1. Very closely related.
2. Quite closely related.
3. Slightly related.
4. Neutral.
5. Slightly unrelated.
6. Quite unrelated.
7. Very unrelated.

The direction of a response depends on one's attitude toward the concept. Respondents should be advised to put their marks in the middle of a space (to avoid confusion) and to make only one mark per scale. They should leave no scale unmarked and should not work back and forth through the items.

UNIT 37
Q Methodology in Social Research

READING:
H. D. Olson and A. G. Gravatt. "The Q Sort as an Attitudinal Measure." *College Student Survey* 2(1968):13-22.

William Stephenson. "Some Observations on Q Technique." *Psychological Bulletin* 49(1952):483-98.

J. R. Wittenborn. "Contributions and Current Status of Q Methodology." *Psychological Bulletin* 58(1961):132-34.

When Q methodology is used in social science research, it requires the use of a kind of factor analysis, a statistical technique that employs correlations and intercorrelations to identify mathematical relationships among variables. For example, factor analysis of a set of semantic differential scales (see Unit 36) might show that several scales represented an underlying dimension accounting for x percent of total variation in scores. Other scales in the set might identify another dimension. For example, some students were asked to evaluate the concept "abortion" on a set of semantic scales. When their responses were tested through factor analysis, it became apparent that they were along two separate dimensions, instrumentality and affect. The first dimension included scales such as "necessary, just, right, humane," etc., while the affective scales were "clean, gentle, caring, considerate," etc. However, in Q method, the factor analysis is different; instead of measuring mathematical relationships among variables, Q factor would tell us that, say, persons 1, 2, and 4 made highly similar responses to choice situations. Hence responses to the sorting of data allows us to categorize the individuals rather than the scales. Initially controversial, Q factor and Q method have been very useful in contributing to the theory of communication.

EXERCISE

What is your favorite television serial?
The question should be very easy to answer, or it might be difficult, depending on how much television you watch. But can you say what your eighth favorite TV show is or the kind of shows you like most, or can you place a single show on the same rating scale with several others? Since there are a lot of TV serials in any season, most people

would be hard-pressed to make choices. This is an example of the kind of situation in which Q methodology helps researchers, and there are many others. Here is a demonstration:

1. Your instructor will list 20 current television serials on the board, or perhaps on a hand-out. Write their titles into the 20 blank boxes provided at the end of this exercise.

2. Cut out the five categories of programs (e.g., romance/drama, situation comedy, etc.) and place them in a semicircle facing you on your desk.

3. Decide which of the five program categories you like best and write the number 1 in the parentheses. Decide your second choice and write the number 2 in the parentheses; do that for all 5 categories. When you have numbered all 5, arrange them in order, 1 to 6, from left to right. Your best-liked choice will be on the left and your least-liked on the right.

4. Now cut out the list of 20 shows (you should have already written titles of the shows in the 20 boxes), and sort them into their appropriate category. Example: The TV serial "The Guiding Light" should be placed in the category "daytime serial." You may place as many or as few show titles as you wish into each category.

5. When you have completed instruction number 4, arrange the TV shows in each category in rank order. Example: Suppose you have five shows in the category "daytime serial"; decide which is your favorite, and designate it "1"; continue with "2," etc.

6. Look back and see if you need to make any further rearrangements. If you decide "daytime serial" was your third most favorite, instead of second, then change it. Be sure all your categories are arranged from most favorite on the far left to least favorite on the far right. But don't labor too long at rearranging because perfection may not be possible.

7. As a final pass, you may reorder the individual program strips. For instance, you may have put situation comedies as your least favorite category, but "Cheers" may be your single most favorite show on TV.

If you remove the category label slips now, you can easily arrange the 20 individual shows into your final order of preference. Put the slips that were arranged from most favorite to least favorite in pile 1 on top of the slips in pile 2, etc. What is left is a pile of 20 TV shows with your first choice on the top and your least favorite choice on the bottom.

In less than 15 minutes you have completed a task that would have taken perhaps a lot of patience and engendered frustration if you had been forced to make your decisions among the 20 shows without the help of Q methodology. Without Q, you might have given up; with Q, it probably was fun.

( ) Romance/drama	( )	( )
	( )	( )
( ) Action/adventure	( )	( )
	( )	( )
( ) Daytime serial	( )	( )
	( )	( )
( ) Situation comedy	( )	( )
	( )	( )
( ) News and information	( )	( )
	( )	( )

UNIT 38 — AAPOR Guidelines

READING:
M. Mark Miller and Robert Hurd. "Conformity to AAPOR Standards in Newspaper Reporting of Public Opinion Polls." *Public Opinion Quarterly* 46(summer 1982):243-49.

The American Association for Public Opinion Research (AAPOR) and the National Council on Public Polls have jointly offered a list of guidelines the mass media should use in disclosing to audiences how polls are conducted. This information is considered the minimum that should be reported with poll stories so that audiences can evaluate the findings being reported. The guidelines, with a short explanation provided where needed, are:

1. Who was the sponsor? Who organized and/or paid for the poll?
2. When was the polling done? How recently? What relevant events were occurring at the time?
3. What was the definition of the population sampled? What group composed the universe for the poll?
4. How large was the sample? How many people or cases were surveyed? What was the completion percentage?
5. How were the interviews conducted? By mail, telephone, or personal interviews?
6. What was the margin of error?
7. Which results were reported by only a portion of the sample? If a finding was based on reports by less than the entire sample, how many cases responded for that finding?
8. What is the exact wording of questions?

A ninth guideline should be added as well: Was the poll based on a probability sample in which every member of the population had an equal chance of being selected for inclusion in the sample? If the poll did not use a probability sample, AAPOR would not include it as a reportable polling procedure.

EXERCISE

It is one thing to read over the list of guidelines and another to use it as a journalist, a researcher, or a communication theorist who is trying to evaluate the strength of a research report. For this exercise, the student is assumed to be a working journalist whose job is to write a news story for a daily newspaper on the following kind of poll:

> The poll was done one week ago to determine if residents of this town would favor a state-approved horse racing track with pari-mutuel betting. The proposal is scheduled for a referendum vote in six weeks. A random sample of telephone numbers in the town's geographic boundaries, with random replacement of the last two phone digits, was done by your school's political science department. A total of 1,465 calls was made to residences between 6 and 9 P.M. The refusal rate was 20%. The key question was: How do you intend to vote on the horse racetrack proposal in the coming referendum? But the question followed a screening question: Do you intend to vote in the coming referendum election? Only 60% of the respondents answered "yes" to the screening question; hence, only those were asked the key voting question. A total of 56% said they would vote for the racetrack.

Write at least the first four paragraphs of a news story on the poll, including all the AAPOR guidelines.

UNIT 39 Choice of Interviewing Method

READING:
Roger D. Wimmer and Joseph R. Dominick. *Mass Media Research: An Introduction*, 2d ed. Belmont, Calif.: Wadsworth, 1987, pp. 119-33.

J. Yu and H. Cooper. "A Quantitative Review of Research Design Effects on Response Rates to Questionnaires." *Journal of Marketing Research* 20(1983):36-44.

One of the early decisions that has to be made in planning survey research is deciding what subject interviewing method to use. How will researchers contact subjects and get them to complete the questionnaire? Should it be by mail, telephone, or in-person interviews?

There are some simple guidelines to go by, which make the decision relatively easy. Here are the chief considerations:

1. Cost. Often cost is the single prevailing factor. If there is little funding available, the decision should be to go with a mail survey. One cost that remains relatively constant in all three interviewing approaches is that of printing or duplicating the questionnaire form.

Admittedly, if the interviewee is going to see the form (either getting it in the mail or looking at it with the help of an interviewer) it should be neater than if read to the interviewer over the telephone. But since all survey forms should be designed in a neat and easy-to-follow manner (we don't want the telephone interviewer to get confused either), they should be well designed. They can be typed and duplicated, as long as they are easy to read. So the cost of the forms is similar regardless of how they will be used. A ballpark figure for producing 1,000 forms might be between $20 and $200, perhaps 20 cents each.

Mail has a definite cost advantage. Once the forms are produced, it costs only two-way postage to complete an interview. So, conceivably, a completed return can be done for under $1, even if there has to be a second mailing to half the subjects. No other interviewing method is as inexpensive as a mail survey.

The phone survey requires having interviewers to make the calls. Even at minimum wage, and the completion of three calls an hour, the cost is greater than mail. Telephone surveys can cost $2 to $5 per completed return, maybe more.

Personal interviews are very expensive to do (so expensive that their cost usually prohibits this interviewing procedure, although personal interviews are superior in almost every other respect. But at $20 to $25 a completed survey, only the well-financed surveys have this option. Personal interviews are expensive because of the interviewers' time and travel. Interviewers have to call each subject for an appointment, travel to the subject's home or office, and must be paid for travel time as well as the time it takes to do the interview. Frequently, the subject breaks the appointment and it has to be rescheduled (and time spent on the no-show also has to be accounted for in overall survey costs).

2. Speed. How quickly does the survey have to be completed? This is another key consideration, particularly for journalistic surveys. If a TV station is preparing a race relations report for its fall ratings sweep and the report has to air next week, there is no decision. The only interviewing approach must be telephone because that is the only way to do a survey in a short period of time. With the help of a newsroom of reporters, a telephone survey could be completed in one or two nights. In-person interviews (with luck and a large staff) might take only two weeks. And a mail survey will require about six weeks to complete.

A mail survey, even if it is sent first class, will take about a week for the first few forms to come back. Then responses will follow the pattern of a normal curve (see Fig. 39.1). Each day more returns

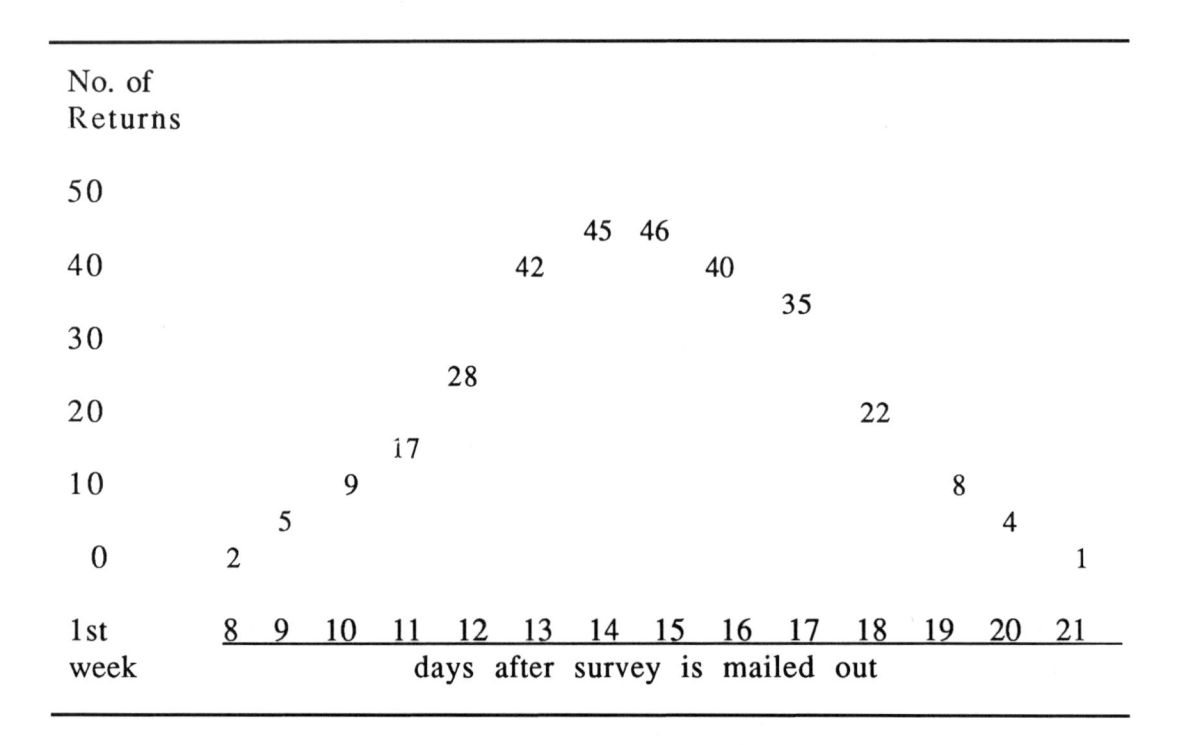

```
No. of
Returns

50
                                    45  46
40                          42              40
                                                35
30
                        28
20                                                      22
                    17
10              9                                           8
            5                                                   4
 0      2                                                           1

1st     8   9   10  11  12  13  14  15  16  17  18  19  20  21
week            days after survey is mailed out
```

Fig. 39.1. Usual response pattern to mail surveys.

will arrive until, perhaps 16 days out, the number is less than the previous days' returns. That drop marks the top of the bell curve and it is all downhill from that point. You might get return envelopes straggling in for three months.

3. Response rate. Depending on the interview method selected, how many of the 1,000 sample subjects are likely to respond? The best approach is personal interviews. With enough funding and tenacity by interviewers, an 85% completion rate is possible. Phone surveys usually get about 75% to 85% completion, although refusals may require beginning with a larger sample of phone numbers.

Mail surveys are notorious for low response rate. Depending on several factors (complexity of the survey form, number of follow-up mailings and the subject's probable interest in the topic), mail surveys may get only a 10% to 30% response rate. While the suggested reading (Wimmer and Dominick) indicates that the average mail survey response is about 50%, we suggest that a response rate this high should be expected only with a research design emphasizing aggressive follow-up procedures and a topic of vital interest to the subject. After all, a direct mail advertising company that could boast of even a 5% response rate would be the industry leader.

4. Length of the survey form (or time needed for an interview). Personal interviews are the best. If the interviewer makes contact (gets face-to-face with the subject) it is possible to have a two-hour session. This means the researcher could collect information on 100 or more questionnaire items. A telephone survey is usually limited to about 10 minutes, although some people will remain on the phone for 45 minutes. Mail surveys must be short. It is unreasonable to expect people to spend more than 10 to 15 minutes completing a mail survey.

5. Complexity of the questionnaire. Again, the personal interview can be extremely complex. With the help of a trained interviewer, the subject can be talked through a variety of scales and complex indices. If the subject doesn't understand, the interviewer can offer guidance or repetitions. The form can even include pictures and graphs. Telephone interviews are limited to verbal responses, but the interviewer does have the opportunity to repeat and explain if the subject gets confused. So while the phone survey has complexity limitations, it can still gather insightful information on a variety of measurement instruments. The mail survey must be the least complex. If subjects become confused about the questionnaire form, it will be tossed in the trash.

6. Assurance that the proper person is completing the survey. The personal interview is best. In a face-to-face interview, there is no doubt that Mr. John Smith is the respondent. Telephone interviews are almost as good (if interviewers are asking for a particular subject by name), but there is always the possibility someone else is on the other end of the line. Mail surveys offer virtually no control over who is completing the form.

While there are a host of more subtle considerations in determining which survey interviewing method to use, these six constitute the main decision points for most survey projects.

One item bears repetition. Often a single consideration (such as needing the survey completed in just a few days or the cost) can determine which interviewing method must be used.

EXERCISES

All things being equal, which of the three survey interviewing methods is used most frequently today? Write a short paragraph explaining your answer.

As a further exercise graduate students might read some journal articles or refer to texts on survey interviewing techniques to come up with a seventh decision point in selecting a survey interview method and compare the relative merit of mail, telephone, and personal interviews on this seventh consideration.

UNIT 40

Validity of Measures

READING:
John Waite Bowers and John A. Courtright. *Communication Research Methods*. Glenview, Ill.: Scott, Foresman, 1984, pp. 118-23.

Validity is a word with both casual and research meaning. (Another such word is *significance*, which in research parlance refers to the chance difference between two or more sets of numbers.) In casual use, you might say, "He had a valid reason for being out of town." Or you might say, "His argument lacks validity." The meaning of the term "validity" might be sufficiently understood, but not precisely. In the examples given above, validity might refer to justifiability, to persuasion, or whatever. But in social science research, validity has special meaning.

Let's define *validity* as the extent to which a research *instrument* measures the variable it was intended to measure. (In social science research an instrument is any measuring device such as a questionnaire, a scale, or an index. A *variable* is any definable property that can vary, for instance, age, marital harmony, extroversion, or conservatism.) Validity is clearly important; how much value would there be in data whose accuracy was unknown? Certainly, we would not want to make important decisions based on faulty measures.

But the definition proposed above is nonspecific. How is one to know whether a measure is valid? If the measure is height or weight, there is no problem; other rulers or scales can verify the outcome. But if the thing measured is more abstract (concepts such as honesty, sympathy, liberalism), the problem of validity is more vexing. Concepts such as honesty, sympathy, and liberalism are not easily validated; they are more likely to be inferred from a set of other behaviors. The challenge, then, is in identifying behaviors or attitudes or perceptions that reflect the variable being studied.

Suppose we wanted to know how liberal the politics of our classmates are; how would we go about creating a valid measure of liberalism? Can you define the term "liberal"? Can you measure its existence in a person? In the space on the next page, try your hand at writing a definition of liberal as it relates to politics. (For example, a liberal is a person who . . . or liberalism in politics means. . . .)

Let's say that liberalism is manifest in both behaviors and attitudes. What behaviors can you think of that are consistent with liberalism? What attitudes?

Behaviors Possibly Associated with Political Liberalism	Attitudes Possibly Associated with Political Liberalism
1. (Example: Individual holds membership in an avowedly "liberal" organization.)	1. (Example: Individual believes government should do more to help its citizens.)
2.	2.
3.	3.
4.	4.
5.	5.

Researchers identify several different types or levels of *internal validity*. One is *face validity*, which suggests that the outcome of a measure can be judged against common expectations. A research instrument has face validity if it appears to the observer to be measuring what was intended. For example, if you were trying to measure "aggression" and you subsequently observed aggressive persons in acts of aggression, you would have face validity.

Another type of validity is *criterion validity*. We might compare a measure with some other accepted indicator of a variable. For example, if we wished to measure "liberalism," we might validate our measure by checking the voting record of persons we identified as liberals. A third type of validity is *concurrent validity*. The word "concurrent" implies "at the same time." For instance, suppose you used several questions to measure a variable; concurrent validity would be suggested by the strong correlations among the several indicators. If you used questionnaire responses to indicate extroversion, then the several responses dealing with extroversion should correlate.

Some textbooks refer to *predictive validity*, the extent to which an instrument predicts a behavior or a relationship among variables. Another type of validity is *construct validity*, which is based in theory. A construct might be "authoritarianism"; such a term is not usually validated by a single study but by an array of studies. The validation, then, is in development of the systematic relationships among selected variables, that is, in the development of theory.

Note also that validity can be external as well as internal. *External validity* refers to the question of whether the research results can be generalized to a broader population.

EXERCISE

Create an example of research that has low internal validity.

Give an example of research that has satisfactory internal validity but low external validity.

Give an example of research that has low internal validity but high reliability.

UNIT 41 — Experimental Design

READING:
Donald Campbell and Julian Stanley. *Experimental and Quasi-Experimental Designs for Research*. Chicago: Rand McNally, 1970, pp. 5-8, 12-14, 24-26.

Much of what has been learned about communication has been learned through a research technique called *experimental design*. Experimental designs provide great control over research variables, and they make it possible to rule out rival explanations of data. Experimental designs usually require hypotheses, which are tested under the strictest of conditions. Strict control is very helpful because in some research methods we can only say that two variables have some kind of relationship (that is, that they vary together), not which one is responsible for the variation in the other.

For example, suppose we are interested in knowing whether reading ability is related to a person's subscription to a daily newspaper. Our hypothesis might be: People who are better readers are more likely to be newspaper subscribers. To test the hypothesis, we would administer a questionnaire to a carefully drawn sample of citizens. Then we could (with their cooperation) test their reading ability. Having done that, we could decide whether a respondent is a good reader or a poor reader. Finally, we could count the subscribers who are good readers and compare them with those who are fair or poor readers. The tabled data might look something like Table 41.1:

Table 41.1. Reading Skill and Newspaper Subscription

	Subscriber	Nonsubscriber
Good Reader	105	18
Fair Reader	65	25
Poor Reader	38	45

Note that we always put the independent variable (the causal variable) on the left; in this case, we are assuming that reading skill is responsible for newspaper subscribership. (It is a questionable assumption; read on.) Looking at the numbers, we see that good readers are likely to be subscribers, and poor readers are not nearly so likely

197

to be. We would compute a chi-square test to learn whether the apparent differences are significant (greater than would be expected by chance variation in a sample).

If the apparent outcome is supported by the statistical test, we might say that good reading skill is related to and apparently causes newspaper subscriptions. That seems plausible, since a poor reader might not be gratified by the labor of reading a newspaper; yet the assumption of causality might be wrong. The numbers really show only a relationship, not a causal variable. For example, suppose the variables of importance actually were education, income, and family experience with newspaper reading. Skill with reading might be only one of several factors leading to newspaper subscribing. Or the relationship of reading skill and newspaper subscription might be more or less coincidental (spurious), not causative.

Experimental methods help to rule out competing explanations of data. In the typical experiment, we would see two or more groups of respondents, which would be matched as closely as possible on relevant criteria (for example, sex, socioeconomic status, education, age, selected attitudes, etc.). In other words, the two groups would be as equal as possible. Then one group would be given an experimental manipulation. That is to say, one group would be exposed to a variable that the other group was not. Suppose Group 1 (children aged 9 to 10) was given a newspaper daily to look at while Group 2 (children of the same age) was not. After two months the groups might be tested for reading skill. Suppose reading scores in Group 1 were significantly improved in comparison with Group 2. If competing explanations were ruled out, we might believe that the newspaper reading improved the children's reading skills. This assumes there were no important intervening variables, events that would alter the outcome of the comparison.

Here is another example. Let's say that we want to test the effectiveness of a particular commercial. We want our respondents to see the commercial and to recall it, but we don't want them to know what we want. (If they knew, it might bias their responses.) To preserve the integrity of the research, we might employ a masking technique; that is, we might recruit people to (supposedly) study a videotaped TV newscast and to rate the newscasters. Unknown to the respondents, we would insert our test commercial into the program. Respondents would then see it more or less incidentally, with no undue focus. After the news show, our questionnaire would ask about the news, but also about the commercials. How much do the respondents recall about the product? About the advertising message? Can they name the product? Its virtues? A word of caution: Researchers must not use damaging deception. Nearly every research institution today has a committee to review researchers' use of human subjects. Researchers must protect the privacy and sensitivity of their respondents.

The experimental method involves manipulation of a variable and use of a test; but often we need another group, a baseline for comparison. The control group serves this function. In some cases the control group and the experimental group are given pretests and posttests because we may need to know whether responses changed from an earlier administration. The risk here is in sensitizing respondents. It is preferred that our respondents be entirely naive about the research, yet a pretest may be necessary.

This brings us to a review of the classic experimental forms, nearly all of which include a control group. Sometimes the design calls for multiple control groups. But in general, control groups, pretests, posttests and post-posttests, and randomization are used to reduce or eliminate threats to research validity. Campbell and Stanley have characterized many of these threats to validity (see assigned reading).

Suppose we have a product, Smile toothpaste, and we want to learn how people react to it. Will they buy it? Let's look at several research designs.

1. Let's say we want to measure the effectiveness of a commercial for Smile toothpaste. We don't want to just show the commercial and ask people what they think; we want to see if the commercial changes their thinking in some way. So let's select a sample of people and separate them into two groups. One group will see the commercial and the other group will not. If the commercial is effective, scores for the two groups should be different. Here is the design:

Randomize into Two Groups	Administer Pretest	Administer Manipulation (show film)	Administer Posttest
Control	Control		
Experimental		Experimental	Experimental

This experimental design allows us to test whether a presumed effect of the commercial is due to some other explanation. The control group represents an estimate of the score of the experimental group in the absence of the manipulation. This design is called a randomized posttest only, with a control group. It does not include a pretest in the experimental condition because that might sensitize subsequent responses.

In this design, would we conclude that the commercial did or did not have the intended effect? If you were conducting the experiment, what competing explanations would you be most concerned with? Assess the design in the space provided below:

2. One problem with the previous design is that it does not take the time factor into account. The passage of time permits the intrusion of intervening variables; things happen that change the responses of some individuals. Suppose the pretest was on January 1 and the posttest was on January 21. Did the participants change in any way during the three weeks? Many things could intervene; one participant may move to Cleveland, or another may have an unfortunate experience with a product similar to the one in the commercial, etc. We have to hope that the change in the individuals is evenly distributed among the groups, but we can build a design to help assure that:

Randomize	Pretest	Manipulation	Posttest
Control	Control		Control
Experimental		Experimental	Experimental

In Design 2, we have added a posttest to the control group. That tells us whether our subjects are likely to have changed over the period of the study; but it has the unfortunate effect of risking instrument sensitization. That is, when the same respondents answer the instrument twice, we are a little unsure of what happens to the scores. That is an element of doubt that we sometimes have to live with.

3. An experimental design that circumvents control group sensitization is given below; it adds a second control group. Notice that the first control group has a pretest, and the second control group a posttest. If the two groups were equal at the outset, this should indicate whether time affected the data.

Randomize	Pretest	Manipulation	Posttest
Control	Control		
Experimental		Experimental	Experimental
Control			Control

4. As you can see, these designs become elaborate. There are several variations, and it is up to the researcher to make the proper choice and the proper justification. The design that is supposed to control for the most possible effects is called the Solomon four-group design given below.

Randomize	Pretest	Manipulation	Posttest
Control	Control		Control
Experimental	Experimental	Experimental	Experimental
Control			Control
Experimental		Experimental	Experimental

Notice that this design has two controls and two experimentals. This accounts especially for sensitization and intervening variables. Since the design requires four groups, it is burdensome. Researchers often don't have the resources and support to use it. But if feasible, this kind of design is highly desirable.

The number of responses needed for an experiment depends on the purpose of the research. If the purpose is to measure an effect, the sample may be small (15 to 30 per group); but on the other hand, if the sample is to be generalized to the broader population, the sample should be large (large enough to accommodate an acceptable error margin and confidence level). Typically, experiments use small samples and surveys use large samples.

EXERCISE

Here is a practical exercise in designing an experiment that could be used in most organizational situations. It should take about an hour to do it well.

As head of the communications or public relations department, you have just done your five-year assessment of employee attitude toward your firm. Yours is a large public utility company, the local gas, electric, and water company. There are 5,000 employees, most of whom are field-workers in installation and repair positions. Your five-year attitude assessment was done with a random survey of 500 employees. The survey shows that employees, particularly the field-workers, don't think much of the company. Morale is lower than it was five years ago, and there is discontent about pay, company policy (where the firm is headed), and lack of communication between management and workers.

You realize something needs to be done to improve employee satisfaction. After all, smoldering discontent can only hurt the firm in the long run, and the field-workers, who are seen most by the public, are your company's front-line representatives. They can either improve or seriously damage your reputation in the community.

The company president and board of directors are concerned about the survey results. You are instructed to come up with a plan to improve employee attitudes toward the firm. You and your staff offer two possible approaches.

1. Create a videotape about the company and its mission. Make it a half-hour show in full color, including top administrators and employee comments about the firm and its mission. Make it upbeat; discuss the points of concern pinpointed by the recent survey. Show the tape to all employees on company time. Have all new employees view the tape as their first assignment. Estimated cost: $50,000. Preparation time: about three months.

2. Organize policy-airing sessions for selected employees in groups of 25 or less. The program will be in a question-answer format, including policy issues and other pinpointed areas of concern. Hold

sessions once a week for a month. The public relations department will organize the sessions with company officials acting as leaders. Bill it as "straight talk with company management." Estimated cost: employee job time and refreshments. Can be ready in two weeks.

The company president opts for the second proposal. If successful, the company may follow up with a videotape later in the year. While the company president likes the policy sessions idea, he does have some reservations. There is the risk the sessions will get out of hand and become confrontations between employees and management, or that employees will consider the sessions a waste of their time. Further, there is no evidence that such sessions will actually result in more favorable employee attitude toward the company. You must demonstrate whether the policy sessions approach will work.

Your department designs a questionnaire to be used as the pretest and posttest to measure attitude change before and after the monthlong sessions. Here are several queries from the questionnaire.

Public Utility Questionnaire

Image Items:	Strongly Agree (5)	Agree (4)	Not Sure (3)	Disagree (2)	Strongly Disagree (1)
1. The firm pays a fair wage for a day's work.	/	/	/	/	
2. Company leaders are concerned about working conditions.	/	/	/	/	
3. This company is a good place to work, compared with other jobs I've had.	/	/	/	/	
4. This utility company would be rated equal to or better than other utility firms in the U.S.	/	/	/	/	
5. Information that comes to me about the firm is understandable and helpful in my work.	/	/	/	/	

The objective is to compare the responses of persons who attend the policy sessions with those of persons who do not attend. Your hypothesis would be something like: Persons who attend the policy sessions will score significantly better on attitudes toward the employer. A wrinkle in the situation, however, is that during the month of your policy-airing experiment, the company announced a 10% pay raise for all employees.

Your task is to develop a research design that would allow you to recommend to your boss that the sessions do or do not effectively improve employee attitude toward the company. The research should be as cost-efficient as possible. Don't waste energy or people's time by setting up an experiment that goes beyond what you need to have confidence in the results.

1. How many employees will you select?
2. How will you achieve randomization?
3. How many groups will you need (experimental and control)?
4. Provide a one-page, typewritten play-by-play description of how you will carry out the experiment (excluding the content of the policy-airing sessions) so that you will be confident that your recommendation to the boss will be accurate.
5. Provide a table of average scores (make them up), which would support the finding that the policy sessions did in fact improve employee attitude toward the utility company.

Index

Advertising, 26
Agenda setting, 84
Ajzen, I., 55
Andersen, K., 72
Animal communication, 111
Antisocial learning, 113
Attitudes, 26, 53
   change, 53
   defined, 53

Babbie, E. R., 123
Balance theories, 62
Ballachey, E. L., 53
Ball-Rokeach, S., 111
Bandura, A., 101
Barnes, A., 75
Bavelas, A., 74
Berelson, B., 3, 11, 75, 80
Berlo, D. K., 72, 179
Bias, 38
Bowers, J. W., 193
Breed, W., 100
Brooks, W. D., 123
Bryan, S., 163
Buckalew, J. K., 22
Budd, R., 75
Bullet theory, 61

Campbell, D., 197
Causality, 198
Chaffee, S. H., 100, 108
Cochran, W., 146
Coding, 174
Cognitive dissonance, 62
Comprehension of text, 160
Confidence level, 149, 152
Connotative meaning, 179
Content analysis, 126, 168
Contingency table analysis, 129
Converse, J. M., 14

Coorientation, 108
Correlation, 84, 127
Credibility research, 72
Cremmins, E. T., 141
Critiquing data, 130
Cronkite, W., 69
Cultivation analysis, 90
Cultural norms, 90

Danielson, W., 163
DeFleur, M. L., 3, 11, 111
Denotative meaning, 179
Dependent variable, 127
Diffusion of information, 75
Diffusion of innovation, 80
Dominick, J. R., 189
Donohew, L., 31
Donohue, G., 43
Doob, A., 90
Dunham, R. E., 73

Emmert, P., 123
Encoding, 160
Encyclopedia, 46
Entropy, 17
Experimental control, 126
Experimental design, 197
External validity, 131

Factor analysis, 72, 138, 174, 184
Fedler, F., 38
Fishbein, M., 55
Flesch, R., 160
Fog index, 165
Freedman, R., 80

Gatekeeping, 22, 143
Gaudet, H., 3, 11, 75

205

Gaziano, C., 43
Gerard, H. B., 53
Gerbner, G., 90
Glynn, C. J., 118
Gravatt, A. G., 184
Gross, L., 90
Group dynamics, 74
Grusin, E., 170
Gunning, R., 163
Gurevitch, M., 96

Hall, J., 38
Hass, H., 96
Headlines, 22
Hovland, C., 65, 69
Hurd, R., 187

Independent variable, 128
Indexing, 7, 180
Information campaign, 58
Information model, 16
Internal validity, 124
Intervening variable, 129
Interviewing, 189

Janowitz, M., 168
Jeffres, L., 75
Jones, E. E., 53
Journal synopses, 141

Katz, D., 53, 54
Katz, E., 80, 96
Kerlinger, F. N., 123, 169
Kidder, L., 155
Knowledge gap, 43
Krech, D., 53

Labovitz, S., 135
Language of sampling, 151
Lasswell, H., 16, 26, 74
Lazarsfeld, P., 3, 11, 61, 75
Leavitt, H. J., 74
Lee, A. Mc., 26
Lee, E. B., 26
Lemert, J. B., 72
Limited effects research, 61
Lippmann, W., 36

McCombs, M. E., 47, 84
McCroskey, J. C., 73
Macdonald, G. E., 90
McGuire, W., 54
MacLean, M., 16
McLeod, J. M., 108, 118
Mandell, W., 65
Margin of error, 152
Measurement in content analysis, 167
Measurement of media use, 7
Media uses and gratifications, 96
Meeske, M., 38
Mendez, A. D., 80
Menzel, H., 80
Merrill, J., 38
Message factors, 65
Meyer, P., 144
Miller, M. M., 187
Models of communication, 16
Morgan, M., 90
Morris, C., 179

Newcomb, T. M., 18
New journalism, 36
News styles, 31
Newsweek, 39
New York Times, 22
Noelle-Neumann, E., 61, 118
Nonhuman communication, 111
Normal curve, 145
Null hypothesis, 125

Observation unit, 151
Operational definition, 127
Opinion leadership, 11
Osgood, C., 179

Pearlin, L. I., 26
Personal influence, 11
Persuasion, 65
Pictures in our head, 36
Piele, L. J., 130
Political socialization, 102
Powerful media, 61
Pre-post test, 129
Presser, S., 14
Propaganda, 26
Prosocial learning, 113
Public opinion polls, 187

Q methodology, 184
Quarles, R., 75
Questionnaire
  analysis, 14
  design, 155
  exercise, 3

Random sample, 128
Rather, D., 69
Readability, 160
Reading ease, 165
Redundancy, 17
Reliability, 124, 131, 168, 174
Research hypothesis, 125
Rogers, E. M., 80
Rosenberg, M., 26
Rubin, A. M., 130
Rubin, R. B., 130

Sampling
  census, 151
  distribution, 151
  element, 151
  error, 125, 131, 144, 152
  frame, 152
  population, 151
  random, 151
  size, 136
  universe, 151
Scott, W. A., 174
Scott's pi, 175
Scripps, H. A., 47
Selective perception, 67
Semantic differential, 179
Shannon, C., 16
Shaw, D., 84
Shoemaker, F. F., 80
Simon, J., 144
Singletary, M. W., 73
Smith, R., 160
Snedecor, G. W., 146
Snider, P. B., 22
Socialization, 100

Social learning theory, 101
Social-psychological model, 18
Source credibility, 69
Spiral of silence, 118
Standard deviation, 150, 152
Stanley, J., 197
Stephenson, W., 184
Stone, G. C., 170
Suci, G., 179

Tan, A., 61, 113
Tannenbaum, P., 179
Taylor, W. L., 163
Theory of relative constancy, 47
Tichenor, P. J., 43
Time magazine, 38
Tipton, L., 100
Two-step flow theory, 3

Use of media, 3, 11, 14
Uses and gratifications, 96

Validity, 131, 168, 193
  concurrent, 195
  construct, 195
  criterion, 195
  external, 195
  face, 194
  internal, 195
  predictive, 195

Wackman, D. B., 108
Ward, L. S., 1
Ware, E. E., 179
Weaver, D. H., 7
Weaver, W., 16
Weiss, W., 69
Westley, B., 16
Wimmer, R. D., 189
Wittenborn, J. R., 184

P 91 .S47 1988

	DATE DUE		